RIDING

RIDING

A Guide for New Riders

Kate Delano-Condax Decker

Lyons & Burford, Publishers

Printed in the United States of America

Design by Marci Kass

10 9 8 7 6 5 4 3 2 1

Library of Congress Cataloging-in-Publication Data

Decker, Kate Delano-Condax.
Riding : a guide for the new riders / Kate Delano-Condax Decker.
p.   cm.
Includes index.
ISBN 1-55821-381-3 (hard cover). — ISBN 1-55821-395-3 (pbk.)
1. Horsemanship.   I. Title.
SF309.D317   1995
798.2'3—dc20   95-6012   CIP

In memory of

"ESSIE"

ESTHER WILSON PERKINS

whose bright, courageous spirit
was the best example
of the best in the
horse world

Contents

Foreword

By Beth Perkins
Olympic Alternate, Combined Training

I CANNOT OVEREMPHASIZE the value of good instruction. Whatever success I have known, I attribute to having had a good horse and good teaching. I've had many teachers, and I would never consider going back into full-time competitive riding without regular help from someone whose opinion I respect. It is important to have someone who will push you, and who will tell you the truth. Compliments have to be earned, not bought.

There are many styles of riding. I think it has been proved that the classical, slow, and consistent approach to riding and training usually wins out in the end. The basics must be firmly learned before one can advance to higher levels, because the sport demands so much of both horse and rider that it will quickly become glaringly apparent if the rider has not done the fundamental work thoroughly. If the confidence of either horse or rider is violated, in most cases the damage between horse and rider is irreparable. Confidence is of utmost importance, and it can only be achieved by building slowly and consistently on a solid foundation.

The value of a book that clearly explains the principles of riding also cannot be overemphasized. It should reinforce your instruction: reading about riding helps you to understand intellectually what is happening physically when you ride. A rider who thinks clearly about what he or she is doing is way ahead of the game. I go back to books whenever I have a problem with my riding, and most of the time it does the trick.

This book explains the fundamentals of riding in clear language that any-one—from beginner to experienced horseman or horsewoman—can readily understand. At the end of each chapter is a quiz to reinforce the reader's understanding and serve as a useful review. There are no shortcuts to riding well. The most important thing is to learn correctly, right from the start. At every level of riding, beginner, intermediate, or advanced, there is plenty of room for improvement, and there will always be lessons to learn. It's a continuing process.

During the three years I trained with Jack Le Goff, coach of the gold medal–winning United States Olympic Team, I must have made every mistake possible. I had a few moments of glory, but along the way I got lost on jumping courses, forgot to take required fences, wore somebody else's number, or forgot to wear one at all, and fell off in Stadium Jumping when I was in first place in an international event. I guess some people have to learn the hard way!

What I remember best about competing during my years with the Team is that when my mother, Essie Perkins, was at an event, the whole atmosphere seemed to change for me. In the heat of intense competition she was always encouraging, and sometimes we would later even be able to laugh at episodes that were at first unbearable. She was devoted to the sport of Three Day Eventing, or Combined Training, because it demands so much of the rider. To be a serious competitor takes integrity, character, talent, and courage. She had all of that, and also a special quality, an extra measure of compassion and gentleness that reached other people and horses too.

Mom competed at Ledyard in the Advanced Division in 1973, a tough competition by any standard, while awaiting surgery for a malignant tumor. She was in pain and had little strength. But I have a picture of her sailing over a fence in Stadium Jumping: she is wearing a huge smile. She was always happy when she was on a horse. She believed you never stop giving your best, and you never stop learning.

—Beth Perkins

Preface

IF YOU WANT TO LEARN to ride with confidence, safety, and good form, this book can help you. It doesn't matter what your age is; people successfully learn to ride at any age. All you need is the right information, presented in the right way, and practice. The enjoyment of riding is far greater if you learn correctly from the start.

Everyone learns at a different pace; no two people master a lesson in precisely the same amount of time. The key to learning and retaining what you learn is this: learn a little bit at a time *correctly* so you will not have to waste time *unlearning* bad habits.

When you are learning to ride, absolutely nothing is more important than finding a good instructor. Although any person of normal intelligence and average athletic ability can learn by hit-or-miss methods to stay on top of a horse, this will not result in an educated horseman or horsewoman. Such a rider will make mistakes that slow down or completely prevent his or her advancing beyond a relatively low level of competence.

Riding can be compared to learning a new language. This language allows you to "talk" with the horse: you can ask questions, make requests, and give orders. This language also allows you to understand the questions the horse asks you, and teaches you the answers to these questions.

This dialogue is conducted through a coordinated system of signals called *aids*. If the system were not coordinated, the signals would begin to interfere with and contradict one another later on during advanced work.

Each aid is a signal that the rider gives by using hands on the reins, legs against the horse's sides, or by changing the placement of weight. Each aid is specific and different from every other aid. Each means something specific to the horse.

A rider must learn each of the aids separately before performing them well enough to combine them for more complex effects. Therefore, a beginning rider first must learn *form*—how to position the body (especially hands, legs, and weight) in order to best apply each aid.

Once a rider is able to sit correctly (and what is correct varies; a rider sits differently when riding uphill from downhill, or when trotting from cantering, for example), he or she learns to apply each aid separately and must practice giving these aids individually until they become automatic.

A rider then learns to combine two or more aids to produce entirely new results. Where the individual aids are like single words, these new combinations of aids are like whole sentences. Using them, horse and rider can "talk": not only can the horse be asked to perform every movement he has been taught, but the rider can teach the horse new work by explaining what he or she wants, using "sentences" the horse already understands. Using this language, the rider can position the horse's body, change his center of gravity, and alter his speed, length of stride, and balance, thereby "speaking" to every part of the horse. In this way, an educated rider can eventually bring out the best movements of which any horse is capable. A rider trained in this way is no longer a mere passenger, but is in full harmony with and control of the horse.

As a new rider, much of your instruction will concentrate on learning good form and the correct use of the aids. This is important because otherwise you will only have to unlearn bad habits later.

This book cannot replace a good teacher. However, it is organized to follow to some degree the procedures that an instructor uses. That is, each new lesson is explained: *what* to do, *how* to do it, and *why* to do it that way. A quiz follows each chapter so you can check your progress.

In every case, you should practice one lesson until you have learned it thoroughly. There is nothing to be gained by moving along too quickly at the expense of learning properly.

A good way to learn thoroughly is to read about what you wish to learn first, then practice the lesson with an instructor, and finally read over the material again. This will help you to better understand and remember it.

Even experts return to their references again and again at different points in their riding careers. This book can serve as your guide to riding with confidence, safety, and good form right from the start.

—Kate Delano-Condax Decker
    1995

1

Taking Lessons

How to Find a Good Instructor

The primary quality to look for in a riding instructor is competence. You must find a person who knows what to teach and who will tell you whether or not you are performing the work correctly. If you can find a teacher with a pleasant manner, so much the better. The ideal instructor is one who combines a high level of competence with a calm, patient, thorough way of teaching. He or she will encourage you to take your time, learn well, ask questions, and never feel that any question you ask is too stupid to answer.

Keep in mind that no one, however skilled a rider, was born knowing what he or she knows now. Everyone has had to learn, and everyone has had to learn at his or her own speed. It is important to learn each lesson thoroughly, and you should find a teacher whose aim is to teach you thoroughly.

Certain highly motivated riders can cope with a teacher who barks orders rather than patiently explains what he or she wants. If you must make a choice between a highly competent teacher with an unpleasant manner and a teacher with a low level of competence and a pleasant manner, choose the former. In such a case, try to listen to *what* is being said rather than the manner in which it is being said. However, if you are looking for an instructor for a child, keep in mind that an unpleasant instructor may turn a child away from riding forever.

How can a beginning rider know if an instructor is competent or not? "Asking around" is not necessarily the best way to find out, because the people you ask may not be the best source of information. Going to a stable that appears well run, where the stalls are clean and the horses well cared for, guarantees you the presence of a good stable manager but not necessarily that of an instructor of the same caliber.

It is best to rely on an established source of information such as the United States Pony Club (or its British counterpart, the Pony Club of Great Britain). The name *Pony Club* is somewhat misleading, because the group's membership includes a large proportion of riders of full-sized horses. The Pony Club, an international organization, explains its primary purpose in its *Handbook*: "To produce a thoroughly happy, comfortable horseman, riding across a natural country, with complete confidence and perfect balance on a pony (or horse) equally happy and confident and free from pain or bewilderment."

Children and young adults up to and including the age of twenty-one are eligible to join the Pony Club and should be encouraged to do so if there is a local club available to join. Moreover, an adult who is a beginning rider can use the Pony Club to obtain reliable information about riding teachers. To find the nearest Pony Club, contact:

United States Pony Clubs, Inc.
4071 Iron Works Pike
Lexington, Kentucky 40511
(606) 254-PONY (7669)

In Great Britain, the British Horse Society is another good source of information. Its address is:

The British Horse Society
National Equestrian Centre
Kenilworth, Warwickshire, CV8 2LR
England

How Much Do Riding Lessons Cost?

Individual lessons generally cost more than group lessons and, if well taught, are worth the difference. Costs vary greatly, depending upon the caliber of the instructor, the locale, and the demand for lessons. If you choose group instruction, try to have no more than one or two others in your class. The benefit of a small group is that you can learn from watching the mistakes of others while still receiving a fair amount of personal attention from the instructor. Try to avoid a large group (six or more), because the instructor cannot give you enough attention and you may form bad habits that will be hard to correct.

The hourly rates for individual lessons vary considerably depending on locale and other factors. One lesson a week from a highly qualified instructor (not necessarily a world-famous one) is of far greater value than several lessons a week from a poorly qualified one. In many areas, you can get well-taught individual lessons for ten to thirty dollars an hour; group lessons cost less. A local Pony Club may be able to give you the names of talented teenage riders who will give you rock-bottom rates and good instruction.

What Kind of Riding Do You Want to Do?

A well-educated rider can get on any horse with any tack and get good performance from that horse. A Western rider, used to using a roping saddle on a horse who neck reins (turns away from light pressure of the reins on his neck), can ride an English horse using a jumping saddle and snaffle bit (a mild, jointed bit used on hunters and jumpers) and feel perfectly at home. In the same way, an English rider can easily ride a Western horse. There are some differences in the aids (signals) used, but whether you ride English or Western, a horse is a horse; he moves according to certain mechanical principles and reacts to signals from his rider with the mind and feelings of a horse. An educated rider may have to learn "what buttons to push" to get certain responses from a particular horse, but will nevertheless quickly be able to ride him well.

The terms *English* and *Western* are catchall words for a number of quite different kinds of riding. English riding, for instance, includes field hunter, show hunter, dressage, three-day-event, three-gaited, five-gaited, pleasure, endurance, sidesaddle, open jumper, breed, steeplechase, racing, gymkhana conformation, and driving. Each of these activities has certain unique characteristics.

In the same way, Western riding includes reining, roping, barrel racing, parade, saddle-bronc, bull-dogging (hazing), pleasure, breed, trail riding, and trail performance.

There is, however, one important practical difference between English and Western riding: it is neither safe nor comfortable for either horse or rider to jump using a Western saddle and bridle. The saddle is too heavy and cumbersome; it strikes the horse's loins on landing after a jump and can damage the horse's kidneys. The bridle, which in most cases is designed to work on a severe leverage principle and is intended for use on a loose rein, can permanently damage a horse's mouth if the rider accidentally falls back on the reins while jumping, Therefore, if you want to learn to jump, you may be well advised to learn to ride with an English saddle and bridle first and, if you wish, take up Western riding later.

As a beginning rider, you should aim to build a good foundation for whatever kind of riding you want to eventually do.

2

A First Horse: Should You Buy, Lease, or Rent by the Hour?

THE BEGINNER may buy a horse, lease one, or rent one by the hour. There are considerations for and against each.

Buying

I f you buy a horse, you will certainly get to know him better than one you lease or rent by the hour. There is something deeply satisfying in knowing that a particular horse belongs to you and you alone. You can care for your horse yourself, if you have the room and facilities, or you can board, or stable, him elsewhere and ride whenever you like. You can name him, clip him, groom him any way you want, and decide who else—if anyone—may ride him. You can take him to horse shows when you are ready, or travel to scenic places to ride him: no one will restrict you from such activities because your horse is needed for other lessons, or because it is against policy.

However, if you are a beginning rider, there are drawbacks to owning a horse too soon. The kind of horse a beginner needs is very different from that needed by an intermediate (which any beginner who applies him- or herself to learning will soon become).

The most important quality in a beginning rider's horse is safeness. This means that the horse's temperament must be docile. He must not be inclined to buck, shy, bite, kick, rear, or bolt; he must not object to being caught in the pasture, trailered (boxed), shod, led, worked around while eating, ridden in traffic, clipped, groomed, bridled, or saddled.

Often, a horse possessing these essential qualities of calmness, obedience, and willingness may not be particularly attractive to look at, thus limiting his future potential uses—as a showhorse, for example. Generally a horse is past his prime or even quite old before he is experienced and quiet enough to be suitable for a beginner. It is a mistake to buy a young horse (three to five years old) no matter how docile he may seem; his nature can change with maturity.

You should face the fact that an older horse's useful years may be few. The time will come when you (or your child) will be ready for an intermediate horse or pony. Since it is not always easy or possible to sell an older animal, if he is very aged, he may have to be retired. If his end comes naturally, it may be hard for your child to accept. He or she may also grow too attached to a pony to part with him, and riding progress may be slowed or halted unless you can afford to keep the pony as a pet and obtain another more appropriate animal.

For any of these reasons, you seldom recoup your expenses in buying a beginner's horse or pony. In addition, your child may outgrow a pony quickly. As the rider's legs must reach the proper point on a horse or pony's sides in order to give the aids correctly, you must not mount your child on too large an animal with the intention that he or she will "grow into it."

However, if you have enough room and are prepared to board and care for a horse properly, you may still want to consider buying your first horse. There is always the chance that someone else will want to buy a beginner's horse when you want to move on to an intermediate one.

WHAT TO LOOK FOR

If you decide to buy a beginner's horse, several factors should be taken into consideration. A beginner should never attempt to buy his or her first horse without expert advice from a qualified person. Again, a local Pony Club, 4-H club, or stable that gives lessons can help find someone to accompany you.

If you are buying a pony for a child, bring him or her along. The child should

SMALL PONIES		LARGE PONIES		HORSES	
10.0 hands	40 inches	12.3		14.3	
10.1		13.0	52 inches	15.0	60 inches
10.2		13.1		15.1	
10.3		13.2		15.2	
11.0	44 inches	13.3		15.3	
11.1		14.0	56 inches	16.0	64 inches
11.2		14.1		16.1	
11.3		14.2		16.2	
12.0	48 inches			16.3	
12.1				17.0	68 inches
12.2					

FIGURE 1:   *Measuring a Horse's Height at the Withers*

try out the pony because a pony that is demonstrated by an experienced child rider may not necessarily be manageable for the beginning child.

Above all, consider the horse's temperament. No matter how appealing he may be in other respects, an animal with the wrong temperament should be rejected. Rule out immediately a horse with any of the vices mentioned earlier: biting, kicking, shying, and so forth. A *mare* (adult female) or a *gelding* (castrated male) is acceptable; a *stallion* (entire, or uncastrated, male over four years) is never acceptable for a novice rider. A *colt* (male under four years) or a *filly* (female under four years) is too young to be considered. Horses ten, twelve, or even fifteen to twenty years of age often make excellent first horses for beginners.

Look for a horse or pony of the right size. Horses are measured in *hands*, a hand being four inches (see figure 1). Ponies may measure up to and including

A.   *Horse too small for rider*

B.   *Horse of proper size for rider*

C.   *Horse too big for rider*

fourteen hands two inches (14.2 hh); horses may reach seventeen hands or more. It is impossible to say how tall a horse should be for a rider of a certain height, because on a broadly built horse a rider's legs will not come as far down the horse's sides as on a narrowly built horse. It is important that the rider's legs hang far enough down the sides of his or her mount to be in the proper position to give the aids. If the rider's feet hang below the horse's belly, however, he or she is too big for the animal (see figure 2).

Try to find a horse that has the maximum number of useful years left. A twelve-year-old horse is better than a fifteen-year-old, all other factors being equal. Keep in mind, however, that the useful life of a horse may extend well into his twenties. The age of a horse can be precisely determined, by examining his teeth, until the age of eight; after that it can be approximated (see figure 3).

Small ponies *may be the right size for many children up to about age twelve.*

Large ponies *may be the right size for many children from thirteen through fifteen years of age.*

A horse of 16 to 16.2 hh *may be the right size for many people of about 5 feet 6 inches in height.*

A horse of 17 or 17.2 hh *may fit a person who is 6 feet or more in height.*

All horses and ponies are measured in hands. A hand equals four inches. A horse who is 15.1 hands is 15 hands one inch; a horse of 15.3 is 15 hands three inches.

Measurements are taken from the ground to the highest point of the withers, using a special measuring stick. (See figure 1)

FIGURE 2:   ***Approximate sizes of horses and ages of riders***

Have the horse examined by a veterinarian for *soundness,* or health. The old saying, "No foot, no horse," is true. Certain unsoundnesses show up only periodically, so you can end up with a chronically lame horse even though he showed no sign of lameness at the time you bought him. A veterinarian can detect subtle injuries and causes of lameness including bone disease.

WHERE TO BUY

The most common places to look for a horse to buy are *advertisements, auctions, riding stables,* and private owners located by *word of mouth.*

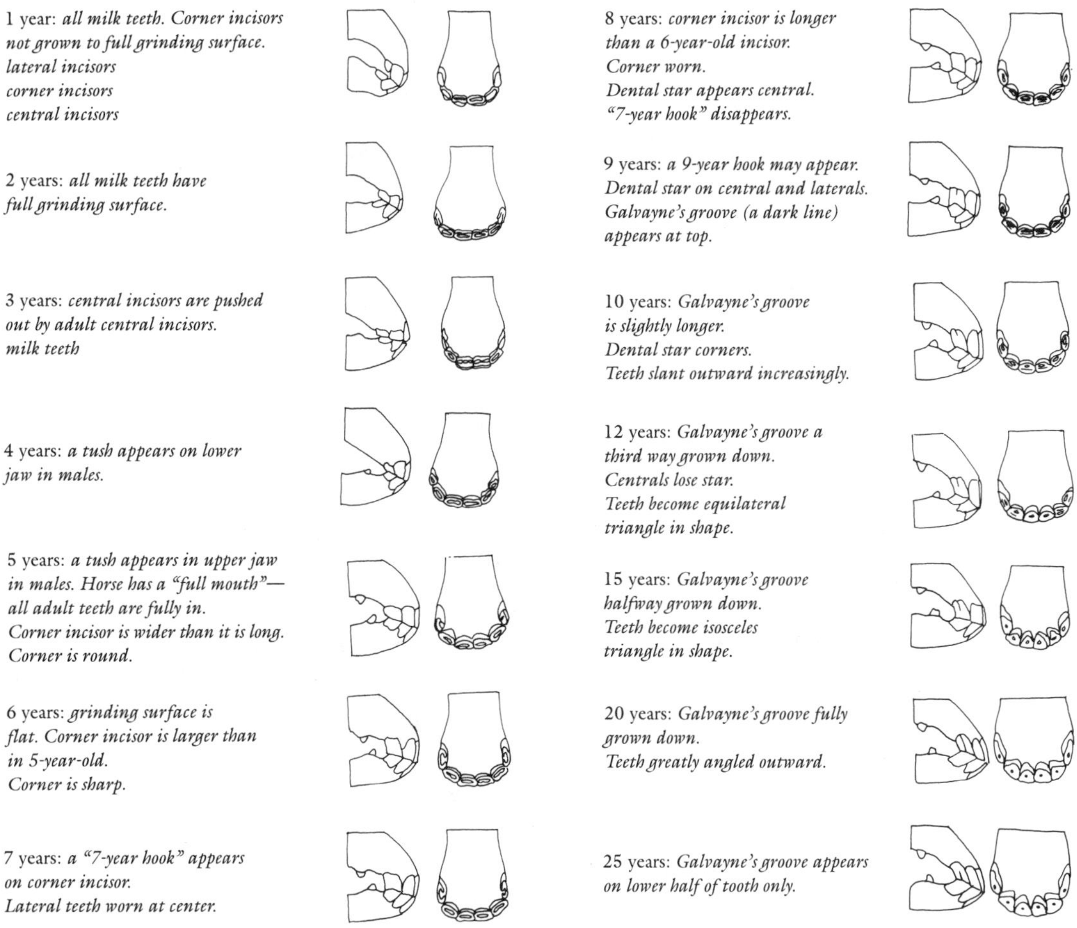

1 year: *all milk teeth. Corner incisors not grown to full grinding surface.*
lateral incisors
corner incisors
central incisors

2 years: *all milk teeth have full grinding surface.*

3 years: *central incisors are pushed out by adult central incisors.*
milk teeth

4 years: *a tush appears on lower jaw in males.*

5 years: *a tush appears in upper jaw in males. Horse has a "full mouth"— all adult teeth are fully in. Corner incisor is wider than it is long. Corner is round.*

6 years: *grinding surface is flat. Corner incisor is larger than in 5-year-old. Corner is sharp.*

7 years: *a "7-year hook" appears on corner incisor. Lateral teeth worn at center.*

8 years: *corner incisor is longer than a 6-year-old incisor. Corner worn. Dental star appears central. "7-year hook" disappears.*

9 years: *a 9-year hook may appear. Dental star on central and laterals. Galvayne's groove (a dark line) appears at top.*

10 years: *Galvayne's groove is slightly longer. Dental star corners. Teeth slant outward increasingly.*

12 years: *Galvayne's groove a third way grown down. Centrals lose star. Teeth become equilateral triangle in shape.*

15 years: *Galvayne's groove halfway grown down. Teeth become isosceles triangle in shape.*

20 years: *Galvayne's groove fully grown down. Teeth greatly angled outward.*

25 years: *Galvayne's groove appears on lower half of tooth only.*

FIGURE 3:   *Estimating a horse's age by examining his teeth*

ADVERTISEMENTS

An advertisement in a horse publication such as *The Chronicle of the Horse* (United States) or *Horse and Hound* (England) or, in some cases, one in the classified section of your local newspaper, usually gives the breed or type, color (see figure 4a, b, c), sex, height, age, and outstanding characteristics of the horse for sale. A typical advertisement might read: "TB ch m, 6 y.o., 16.1 good mover. 1st yr. green," which translates as: Thoroughbred, chestnut-colored mare, six years old, sixteen hands one inch high at the withers, with an attractive way of moving that will be pleasing to horse-show judges, and eligible to enter in classes at shows that require horses to jump fences up to three feet six inches in height.

Unfortunately, horses suitable for beginners are infrequently advertised in magazines and newspapers because their lower selling price does not warrant the cost of an advertisement. However, if you can find one, such an advertisement might read: "Roan gelding, 14.3, 11 yr., sound, quiet, excellent for novice," which means reddish-colored, gelded (castrated) horse, not lame, gentle. Be prepared to add a few years to the given age of such a horse, as sellers often give an old horse the benefit of the doubt to a rather generous degree. If the advertisement seems promising, a telephone call can help clarify any questions you have. If you must travel a substantial distance to examine the horse, you may first want to see a photograph; it is reasonable to request one by mail before you make a long trip.

When you go to try out the horse, be sure to take along an expert; do not attempt to choose your first horse unadvised. Most people selling horses are reasonably honest, but horse dealing is notorious for pitfalls into which the unwary or uninitiated may stumble. There are unscrupulous sellers in this field,

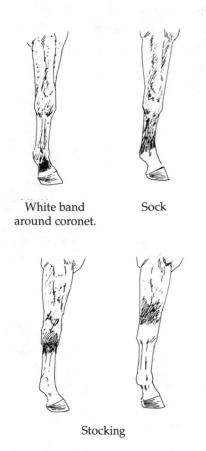

White band
around coronet.

Sock

Stocking

FIGURE 4A: *White Markings on Legs*

Try out the horse thoroughly at the seller's stable. Both the expert accompanying you and the person for whom the horse is being purchased should ride him. The expert should walk, trot, canter, gallop, stop, turn, and back the horse, as well as take him over a small fence if the horse has been advertised as able to jump. If possible, take the horse out of a ring or enclosed area and try riding him away from the stable alone to see whether he becomes balky or disobedient when taken away from the barn and other horses. The expert should look at the horse's *conformation* (body shape

as in any other sort of business. Here are some ways in which you can get as much accurate information as possible.

FIGURE 4B: *Colors of Horses*

Because horses had few defenses against their enemies except the ability to run, they developed protective coloration. Consequently, there is a wide variety of colors in horses seen today.

Dark gray: dark gray hair, black skin

Dappled gray: mottled pattern of light and dark gray

Fleabitten gray: white or gray hair with brown specks all over

Light gray: hair with age becomes almost white, but skin remains black

Black: jet black hair and skin

Dark brown or Seal brown: blackish brown hair all over, light skin

Bay: dark brown body, black mane, tail, legs, muzzle

Liver Chestnut: darkish brown liver color all over

Chestnut: reddish brown to medium or light brown all over

Palomino: golden color, white mane and tail, sometimes white stockings or socks

White: hair pure white; skin pink; sometimes has one or both blue eyes

Strawberry roan: red hair with individual white hairs mixed throughout

Blue roan: gray-brown hair with white hairs mixed throughout

Appaloosa: dark body of brownish, grayish, or reddish color, with white spots. "Blanket" pattern appears on rump only; "Leopard" patterns appears all over.

Dun: yellowish color body with black legs, mane, tail; usually also muzzle and dorsal stripe along spine.

Piebald: black marking on white

Skewbald: brown markings on white

Sorrel: reddish brown body, "flaxen" (lighter color) mane and tail; term is usually applied to western horses

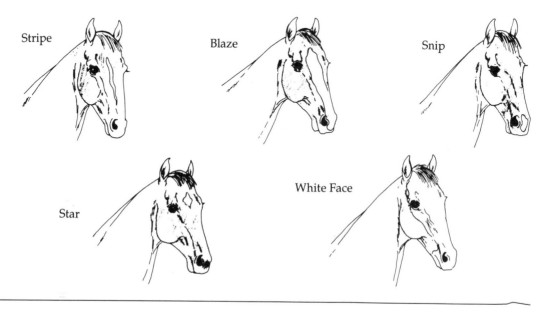

Stripe

Blaze

Snip

Star

White Face

FIGURE 4C: *White Markings on Face*

and proportions) (see figures 5 and 6). Ask questions; most sellers will tell you the truth if you ask, but will not volunteer information they believe will jeopardize the sale. The expert you have brought will be of invaluable assistance in asking the right questions, such as specific inquiries about the horse's temperament, behavior under various circumstances, conditions, and past history. In rare instances, a seller will allow you to take the horse home for a week's trial, which is ideal.

If you like the horse after you've given him a thorough trial, arrange to have a veterinarian check him before any money changes hands. It goes without saying that you should never buy any horse not sound of wind and limb. Sometimes the seller will give you the name of a vet in the area, or you may have your own vet examine the horse, but do not have the horse examined by

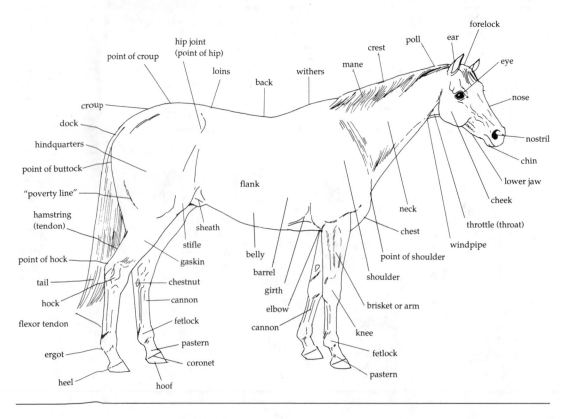

FIGURE 5: *Parts of the Horse*

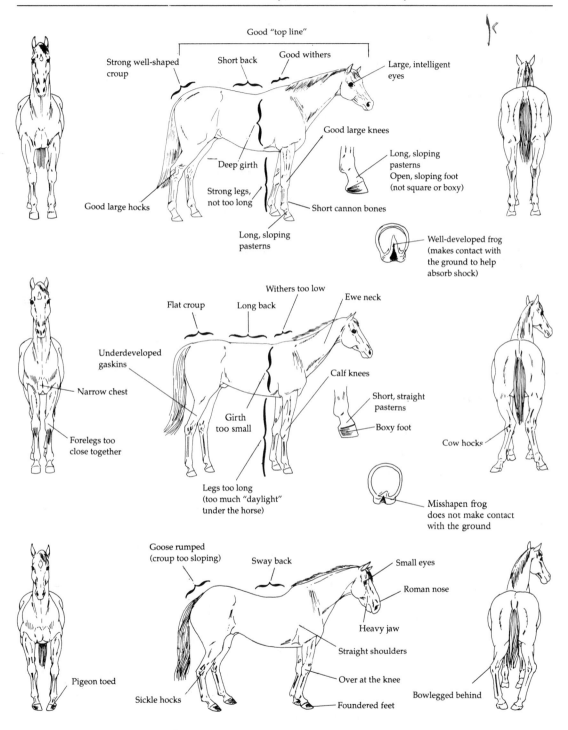

FIGURE 6: *Conformation*

the seller. If the horse is sound, the examining veterinarian will give you a written, dated certificate. At this time you can arrange to pay the seller and the vet, who will charge a moderate fee for his or her participation.

The usual time to pay is when the horse leaves the seller's premises. Most sellers want cash or a certified check, although the method of payment is negotiable. Normally, no warranty or guarantee is given. If the horse turns out to be disappointing in any way once you have taken possession of him, the seller is under no obligation to take him back or return the purchase price. The rule is to look long and hard, and, finally, to buy carefully.

AUCTIONS

If you buy at an auction, you can usually see and try out the horse beforehand. Many useful horses and ponies change hands this way. However, an auction may be the riskiest place for a novice to purchase a horse, for many reasons. The conditions under which you try out the horse are far from ideal: the riding area may be limited in size, and the confusion of the surroundings can daze the horse, making it difficult for you to learn his real nature. There is usually no one to answer detailed questions about the animal. Auction employees may have fewer compunctions than the owner would about stretching the truth on the merits of a horse offered for sale. Some unscrupulous people drug an unruly horse before an auction to make him appear docile.

Before you pay for a horse you have decided on at auction, it is wise to have him examined by a qualified veterinarian (as you would in a private sale). Some auctions have already had the horse vetted, and the certificate of examination is then kept by the auctioneer, to be inspected by potential buyers. However, it is advisable to use a veterinarian you know has no connection with the auction. Usually, no other warranty is given with any horse purchased at an auction; even when one is, it is usually of very short duration, sometimes only a few hours.

All things considered, the chances are greater that a buyer will purchase a horse with hidden flaws at an auction than through any other method of purchase. Nonetheless, good horses *do* pass through auctions, and the major reason to go to an auction at all is the possibility that you may find a genuinely good animal at a bargain price.

Sometimes the auction has delivery service available for a fee; otherwise you should come prepared to haul your horse home yourself, or to return for him within twenty-four hours.

RIDING STABLES

Riding stables are one of the best places to buy a first horse. The advantages are many. You can try out a horse thoroughly before purchasing. A reputable stable wants to protect its reputation and is therefore more likely to take extra care to sell you only a horse with which you will be happy, particularly if you are a student at its riding school.

However, some riding-school horses become so used to being ridden only with other horses in lessons that they are balky and disobedient when ridden alone. Be sure to try out the horse both in company and alone, and to have a qualified expert advise you.

The main disadvantage to buying a horse from a riding stable is that it may cost more than purchasing from an individual owner (to whom a good home may be more important than price) or from an auction.

WORD OF MOUTH

Perhaps the best source from which to buy your first horse is a member of the Pony Club. With their emphasis on good sportsmanship and fair play, Pony Club riders are the people least likely to misrepresent a horse. Some Pony Clubs keep a list of horses for sale, and the District Commissioner (head) of a particular Pony Club can sometimes help you find a horse that is suitable for a beginning rider. Once the word is out that you are looking for a particular kind of horse, the chances are good that you will sooner or later hear from someone with just that kind to sell.

4-H clubs, located throughout the United States, can also offer guidance.

As in every case of buying a horse, try the horse thoroughly before purchasing, bring an expert along with you, and have the horse vetted.

PRICES OF HORSES

The prices of horses vary widely, due to factors that include the horse's breed; size; age; geographic location; condition; level of training; and proven ability as a show horse, child's pony, or whatever. That age-old factor, "what the traffic will bear," also plays a role. If more than one potential buyer is interested in a particular horse, the price is apt to go up. Read advertisements in local newspapers and horse magazines like *The Chronicle of the Horse* (published in Berryville, Virginia) and look at horses for sale in several stables to get an idea of the going price for the kind of horse you are interested in. Bargaining is very much a part of horse dealing, and if you are careful to keep the tone pleasant and friendly, you can often gain a concession in price. Stress any factors in your favor, such as a willingness to give the horse a good home, or the fact that a child will be riding the horse under an instructor's supervision. If you are close to reaching an agreement, sometimes offering slightly less than the asking price, in cash, will close the deal.

Leasing

Some stables allow a prospective buyer to lease a horse for a month or longer to try him out thoroughly before purchasing. Also, a horse can sometimes be leased without the intention of purchasing. This arrangement may suit the owner in cases where he or she is unable to spend adequate time with the horse and may want someone reliable to ride and tend to him. The period of time that you lease the horse may be decided upon by mutual consent in advance on a month-by-month basis. During the leasing period, the owner will charge you—the lessee—a set fee, which varies greatly depending upon the value of the horse and the locale. An expensive horse will probably cost more to lease than an inexpensive one, and a horse leased in a major city will probably cost more than one leased in the countryside.

In addition to the cost of leasing the horse, you may also be required to pay his board for the duration of the lease. Boarding costs also vary considerably, and it is difficult to give an "average cost" figure. Assume that leasing a horse who is pleasant to ride but has no outstanding show potential might cost you $300 to 400 per month at a major stable in a city, plus $300 to 400 per month to board, bringing your costs to upwards of $700 per month. The same sort of arrangement in a countryside area where horses are plentiful might cost much less. Leasing and boarding costs depend upon what the market will bear, so if you do decide to lease, it pays to shop around.

Some stables do not like to lease a horse normally used for riding lessons, even if you are reasonably sure that you will buy him when the leasing period is up, because it takes a popular horse out of riding-school circulation. Other stables like to lease horses, to generate income that they would not otherwise get.

If you lease with an option to buy, make sure that the leasing fees (and boarding fees, if possible) will be applied toward the purchase price if you eventually decide to buy the horse. Have the purchase price specified in writing. Also be certain that in the event of any injury to the horse, the owner, not you, will assume full responsibility. Settle both matters with clear statements in writing, signed by both the owner and you, with a copy retained by each. In the event of a dispute, your written statements will determine the extent and nature of your obligation.

Leasing a horse with the clear understanding that you have no interest in purchasing has the advantage that you will be able to return him to his owner at a certain time without going to the trouble of putting him up for sale. Be sure to get a written agreement spelling out what you will be responsible for, and what responsibility the owner agrees to assume.

If you as rider are injured, you will bear the responsibility for your own injuries; if the horse you are riding is injured, the owner will assume responsibility unless he can prove that the injury was due to your negligence or wanton disregard of stable regulations.

Renting by the Hour

Renting a horse by the hour without instruction is the least effective way to learn to ride, and is not recommended. The horse you rent has been ridden by many other people, and has probably learned bad habits from poor riders. Also, you will not have the opportunity to spend enough time with him to get to know him well.

If you do rent and ride a horse by the hour at a public stable, remember to look for signs, usually prominently displayed, stating the stable's rules. If such a sign is clearly displayed, you may be held legally responsible for abiding by these rules—whether or not you read them.

Breeds

There are perhaps as many breeds of horses as there are breeds of dogs. Each breed has certain characteristics that are common to most, although not all, its members. For example: Shetland ponies tend to be docile and quiet, while Welsh ponies tend to be more lively; Thoroughbreds and Arabians tend to be fleet and agile, while Percherons and Clydesdales move more slowly and heavily; and so forth. However, there are exceptions to the rule in any breed.

How did different breeds come about?

Millions of years ago, *Eohippus*, a four-toed animal the size of a small dog, lived in North America. Since it had no defenses against its enemies except protective coloration and the ability to run, it was constantly on the alert for danger. It developed great speed by running on its toes. Over a long period of time, the middle toe evolved into a larger and tougher toe than the others, which became smaller and finally all but disappeared. (Today, these vestigial toes form the horse's fetlock.)

Equus, the first horse to closely resemble the horse of today, lived first in North America and later, driven by the ice age, in South America, Asia, Africa, and Europe—then joined by land bridges. Modern breeds developed from the *Equus* on each of these continents.

In barren, cold Asia, food was scarce. Tough, small, shaggy ponies survived the bitter winters, and among their descendents are the *Przhevalski's horse*—a small dun-colored pony that today exists only in captivity—as well as other donkeylike, pony-sized animals.

In Africa, a lightly built, fleet horse developed on the grassy plains and became the ancestor of most of the light breeds today used for riding. The *Arabian* and the *Thoroughbred* are typical of these breeds.

Europe produced big, strongly built horses which were later used by armored knights and from which are descended today's draft breeds, such as *Percherons*, *Clydesdales*, and *Shires*.

Ponies developed on islands off Europe and in isolated places where food was scarce. They resemble miniature versions of the breeds from which they originated: the *Shetland pony*, for instance, is built like a tiny draft horse.

In the 1500s, Spanish explorers brought a number of horses of the Arabian type from Spain to Mexico. Some of these ran wild and formed the bands of horses that flourished to produce, eventually, the *mustangs* of the west. Their descendents, tamed by the American Indians, had grown smaller and tougher while running wild for generations.

People discovered that if they bred mares with stallions who possessed exceptional qualities, they could produce offspring that had superior characteristics; thus selective breeding came into existence. The record of a horse's ancestry is called his *papers*.

The ancestry of the Arabian horse can be traced back for more than two thousand years. Strong, intelligent, and fast, standing about fifteen hands high, the Arabian of today is the product of thousands of generations of careful breeding.

The term *Thoroughbred* is often misunderstood. Thoroughbred is the name of a particular breed; it does *not* mean *purebred*. The Thoroughbred was the result of crossing European mares with Arabian stallions. Every Thoroughbred can be traced back to one of three Arabian *sires* (stallions) who established the breed around 1700. Bigger than the Arab, the Thoroughbred can reach seventeen hands or more, sixteen hands being average. Among the most spirited of breeds, the Thoroughbred can become excited, or "hot," if improperly handled.

Because of its long stride and great speed, the Thoroughbred has become today's race horse. It can reach speeds of forty miles per hour at the gallop.

The Puritan colonists disapproved of racing, which meant competing at the gallop, but since technically they were not prohibited from letting their horses *trot* as fast as they could go, farmers often used to have an undeclared, friendly trotting race whenever one just "happened" to draw alongside a neighbor's buggy on a quiet country road. From the horses of these colonists came *Standard-breds*, the trotters and pacers of today.

When a Thoroughbred is bred to another purebred horse, the term *Anglo* is prefixed; an Anglo-Arab is a Thoroughbred-Arabian cross. A horse that has one purebred parent is called a *half-bred* horse. A horse with very little purebred blood is called a *grade* horse and one with little discernible breeding is called a *cold-blooded* horse. Having some recognizable signs of good breeding can add to a horse's appearance and value. Such a horse is often referred to as "typey," meaning he is not purebred but does have something of a purebred's refined "type."

In Europe, horses that were both strong and fast were needed to pull stage-coaches. By crossing draft breeds with Thoroughbreds, the *Cleveland Bay* and the *Hackney*, among other coach breeds, were developed.

The *American Saddle Horse* was developed from a Thoroughbred stallion in the 1800s by Kentucky plantation owners. These breeders wanted a horse that was showy, with energetic action, but calm and comfortable to ride while inspecting their estates.

The *Morgan* breed was founded by a sturdy, short-legged, muscular little horse of unknown ancestry owned by a schoolteacher named Justin Morgan in the 1700s. Possessing great courage, stamina, and intelligence, the first Morgan horse passed these qualities along to his offspring.

The *Tennessee Walker*, later used by plantation owners, was bred by crossing Saddlebreds with Morgans.

The *Quarter Horse*, descended from a Thoroughbred sire in colonial times, was prized for its ability to run fast for a short distance. Somewhat similar in appearance to a Thoroughbred, but smaller and more muscular, the Quarter Horse was the product of crossing Thoroughbreds with the small, tough mustangs that descended from horses brought by the Spaniards in the 1500s. More recently Quarter Horses have been selectively bred for great beauty, endurance, and stamina.

There are many breeds of horses and ponies in addition to these. The important thing to note is that a purebred horse is not necessarily a better horse than one who is not. A horse with good conformation and a calm disposition is a sound investment, whereas a horse with papers, but poor conformation and a hot temperament, is not a good choice. So when you are looking at a horse with the thought of buying, make your choice on the basis of his soundness, temperament, and conformation, not merely his papers or attractive appearance.

QUIZ

1. *True or false:* Your first horse should always be purchased at the same time you begin riding.

2. Name ten parts of the horse that are located in front of the saddle.

3. Name ten parts of the horse that are located behind the saddle.

4. The color of a horse with white hair but dark skin is
   (A) white
   (B) roan
   (C) gray

5. Arrange the following in order of size, putting the largest white area first:
   (A) blaze, stripe, snip, bald or white face, star
   (B) stocking, band, sock

6. Horses are measured in
   (A) hands
   (B) feet
   (C) inches

7. The term *16.2 hh* means that a horse is
   (A) sixteen hands two inches tall measured at the back
   (B) sixteen hands two inches tall measured at the withers
   (C) sixteen feet divided by two, or eight feet long from head to tail

8. Which quality is most important in a first horse?
   (A) age
   (B) temperament
   (C) appearance

9. Why shouldn't you buy a three-year-old pony for a child even if the pony's nature is very docile?
   (A) His nature may change as he matures.
   (B) Most children should have lively first ponies.
   (C) A docile nature is least important in a child's first pony.

10. A horse that is correctly proportioned without any serious faults in his body shape is said to have
    (A) a "hunter" look
    (B) good impulsion
    (C) good conformation

11. At what age does a horse have a "full mouth" of all adult teeth?
    (A) four
    (B) five
    (C) eight

12. When you try out a horse, you should *always* take along
    (A) a saddle
    (B) a snaffle bridle
    (C) a qualified expert

13. *True or false:* It is important when leasing a horse to get the agreement in writing and to be certain that, in the event of injury to the horse, the owner, not the rider, is responsible.

14. Regarding lessons, the *two* most important things are to
    (A) take lessons at a reputable stable
    (B) take lessons from a qualified instructor
    (C) ride the same horse every day
    (D) take group lessons at first, and only transfer to private lessons after a few weeks

15. The written record of a purebred horse's ancestry is called his
    (A) breeding
    (B) papers
    (C) track record

16. *True or false:* It is always best to buy a purebred horse, not a grade or cold-blooded one.

17. *True or false:* The term *Thoroughbred* means "purebred."

Answers: 1. false. 2. forelock, ear, eye, poll, crest, forehead, muzzle, nose, nostril, lips, chin, cheek, throat, neck, mane, shoulder, withers, girth, elbow, forearm, knee, cannon, fetlock, coronet, pastern, hoof, heel, ergot, chestnut. 3. flank, back, loins, point of croup, croup, dock, tail, buttock, poverty line, stifle, gaskin, hock, sheath, cannon, chestnut, fetlock, ergot, pastern, coronet, hoof, heel. 4C. 5A. bald or white face, blaze, stripe, star, snip. 5B. stocking, sock, band. 6A. 7B. 8B. 9A. 10C. 11B. 12C. 13. true. 14A,B. 15B. 16. false. 17. false.

3

Riding Clothes

What the Rider Should Wear

The safest and most comfortable clothes for riding are those that were designed for the purpose.

A *hard hat* (also called *helmet* or *hunt cap*) is necessary for every rider. Get the kind with a safety harness that fits across your chin and behind your head, and that can later be removed to convert the cap to a regulation hunt cap suitable for hunting or showing. This costs from twenty-five to sixty dollars or more. No substitution can be made for this essential piece of equipment. Every rider sometimes has falls, and a safety helmet will prevent a head injury.

If possible, invest in *breeches* (pronounced "britches") and high boots, as these best protect your legs from discomfort. Breeches are reinforced at the knee with an extra layer of cloth or a suede patch that protects your knee from chafing by the stirrup leather. Plain cotton/nylon stretch breeches are easy to mount in, washable, and cost from $30 to more than $100. They should fit snugly, particularly over your calf, where they must be tight enough so as not to ride up.

High leather boots serve to protect your calf. They should be either black or brown (black is formal; brown informal). *Field boots* are brown, mahogany-colored, or black, with laces over the instep like a shoe. They should be as tall as possible when you buy them—right up to or even slightly above the back of your knee joint—as they will drop two inches when the leather at the ankle breaks in. The leg must not be tight, but it should fit snugly. If you can slide no more than one or two fingers between the boot and your calf, the fit is ideal. However, the foot should be comfortably loose so that you can wear an extra pair of socks for winter riding.

Another good and often less-expensive option is *jodhpurs* (pronounced "jod-purs") and *jodhpur boots*. Jodhpurs fit snugly to the ankle and are worn with ankle-length leather jodhpur boots.

Rubber boots in black, brown, or *Newmarket style* (tan canvas top with brown foot) protect your leg fairly well, but they prevent moisture inside from evaporating, and tend to be hot in summer and cold in winter. They are easy to care for—just rinse them off with water—and considerably less expensive than leather ones. Ready-made leather boots may cost from $100 to 250 or more—with prices continuing to increase—while rubber ones are a fraction of that. However, leather boots, if kept clean, treated with saddle soap, and stored on boot trees, will last for many years, while rubber ones may last only a year or two.

Hacking jackets (informal) and formal black *hunt coats* should be of wool for winter, and of cotton/synthetic fiber materials for summer. They cost from fifty to several hundred dollars. They are necessary for showing, but not for general riding.

Pony clubs, riding clubs, and riding stables sometimes have secondhand riding clothes for sale; this may be worth looking into, particularly in the case of children, who outgrow clothes quickly. Local tack shops and catalogues sell clothing as well.

If you do not want to buy breeches and boots immediately, wear tight-fitting jeans with straight legs (not flare-bottoms). Wear long underwear underneath (for winter) and knee socks that will stay up around your calf (for both summer and winter). Do not use streetwear boots with zippers along the inside of the calf; these will chafe your legs. Do not use any boots or shoes without heels, such as sneakers (plimsols), as your foot could go through the stirrup and you could get dragged in the event of a fall. Wear lace-up leather shoes with a one-inch heel, or cowboy boots if you have them, with the tops worn under the jeans, not the jeans tucked into the boot tops. However, unless cowboy boots are tall enough to protect your calf, the stirrup leathers may chafe.

You need not buy a hacking jacket (riding coat) initially, since any warm jacket short enough to clear the saddle will do for winter (a hip-length, ski-type parka, which is both light and warm, is especially good), and a simple shirt or sweater is fine for summer.

Never wear trailing scarves, coats that are too long to clear the saddle (except for a riding mackintosh especially designed for riding on rainy days), high-heeled shoes or boots, or mittens or gloves made of wool (unless they have leather palms; otherwise they slip on the reins). For everyday riding your appearance should be workmanlike, and jewelry should therefore not be worn. If you have long hair, it should be tied back or kept in a hairnet. Dress codes for participation in horse shows, however, are strict (see figure 7).

If you need help in finding a tack shop that sells boots, hard hat, and breeches, ask a riding stable or Pony Club for the name of the nearest one. You might also contact riding-supply companies that sell by catalogue. Miller Harness Company is especially good. You can contact them at 1-800-553-7655. Your local library can give you the names and addresses of others.

Show Rider—Adult

Hard hat—black

Choker (usually patterned or colored)—informal; white stock tie—formal.

Plain shirt, standard collar-less band that buttons snugly at neck

Jacket—formal: *solid dark color (navy, burgundy, brown);* informal: *patterned (herringbone, checks, muted plaid)*

Gloves—leather or string

Breeches (tan, beige, or "canary" pale yellow)

Boots—formal: *black leather with black patent leather tops for women, black leather with tan tops for men (tabs sewn on, but not down)* optional; informal: *field boots (laced at instep like a shoe) in black, brown, or mahogany color.*

Derby—required for adults who foxhunt

Rubber boots—black or "Newmarket style" (tan canvas with brown rubber)

Show Rider—Child

Jacket—solid or patterned

Straps to prevent jodhpurs from riding up

Jodhpurs (tan or brown)

Jodhpur boots (brown)

Hard hat—black with chin strap

Riding Clothes: What to Wear If You Can't Buy the Standard Clothes Right Away

Any kind of jacket short enough so it just reaches the saddle when the rider is mounted.

String or leather gloves (not woolen ones, which slip on reins).

Tight-fitting jeans (not loose ones, which chafe and ride up).

Lace-up shoes with 1-inch heels—not rubber soled, which can get caught in stirrups.

Leather schooling chaps—to protect legs. Should fit snugly, but not tightly, all over. May be "roughout" (sueded) or smooth leather.

FIGURE 7: **The Rider's Clothing: What to Wear**

QUIZ

1. The one item of riding clothing that every rider *must* wear is
   (A) high boots of either black or brown leather
   (B) a hard hat
   (C) regulation breeches in tan or brick color

2. The word *breeches* is pronounced to rhyme with
   (A) peaches
   (B) ditches

3. Short leather boots for riding are correctly pronounced
   (A) jod*ph*ur boots (pronounced with an "f" sound)
   (B) jod*p*ur boots (pronounced with a "p" sound)

4. One pair of high leather boots is black, the other brown. Which is considered formal?
   (A) black
   (B) brown

5. High boots with a tan-colored canvas leg and brown foot in either leather or rubber are called
   (A) Newmarket boots
   (B) ready-made boots
   (C) Wellington boots

6. Three items of clothing no rider should wear are
   (A) a short nylon parka
   (B) flare-bottom jeans
   (C) lace-up shoes with a one-inch heel
   (D) sneakers or plimsols
   (E) cowboy boots
   (F) woolen mittens

7. The correct fit for new high leather boots before they have been broken in by riding is
   (A) loose in the calf and tight in the foot
   (B) snug in the calf and tight in the foot
   (C) comfortably loose all over
   (D) as tall as possible, up to or slightly above the back of the knee joint

8. High brown, mahogany-colored, or black leather boots that lace over the instep are called
   (A) jodhpur boots
   (B) field boots
   (C) hunt boots

Answers: 1B, 2B, 3B, 4A, 5A, 6B,D,F, 7D, 8B.

4

Tack and Equipment

A BEGINNING RIDER need not own any *tack* (the equipment worn by the horse) unless he or she owns a horse, but all riders should have a working knowledge of the bridle, saddle, and martingale, and know how they should fit both rider and horse. In addition, all riders should be familiar with various kinds of whips and know how to use them.

The Bridle

The *bridle* holds the bit in the horse's mouth. It must be kept clean, so it does not chafe, and properly adjusted (see figure 8). The *bit*, lying snugly but not tightly in the horse's mouth, gives signals (*aids*) to the horse from the rider's hands through the reins.

The bit is made of stainless steel or nickel and is sometimes covered with rubber where it lies in the horse's mouth. The two principal kinds are the *snaffle bit* and the *curb bit*.

The snaffle is milder than the curb, and works on a direct-action principle: the amount of pressure that the rider puts on the reins is the amount that the horse feels on the bit. There are various kinds of snaffles; several of the com-

Bridle Adjusted Too Tightly

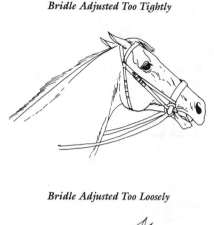

Crownpiece or headpiece

Browband

Cavesson or noseband

Cheek piece

Throatlatch

Plain reins

Bridle Adjusted Too Loosely

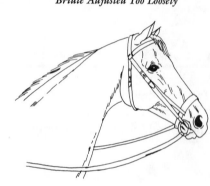

FIGURE 8: *Bridle Properly Adjusted*

mon ones are shown (see figure 9a). Most snaffles are jointed in the middle of the part that lies in the horse's mouth. Such jointed snaffles work gently on the corners of the mouth. A refined signal can thus be given to the horse, since pressure can be applied, when desired, to only one side of his mouth at a time.

The bit should be wide enough when it is in the horse's mouth so that it does not pinch the corners of his mouth inward.

The curb bit works on a leverage principle: the pressure that the rider puts on the reins is intensified many times when it is felt by the horse. Even a small tug on the curb reins is felt by the horse as greatly increased pressure. The *shanks* of a curb bit, combined with a *curb chain*, which fits under and just behind the horse's chin, exert pressure, tending to make him "bow" his head and tuck in his chin. The longer the shanks are, the greater the leverage pressure. The curb also tightens the *cheekpieces* of the bridle, which exert pressure on the *crownpiece*. If a *port* (see figure 9b) is included in a curb bit, it increases the bit's

Some of the most common kinds of bits that work on the curb principle.

Eggbutt snaffle

Rubber snaffle

Full-cheek or Fulmer snaffle
(cheek pieces prevent pulling
through mouth to side).

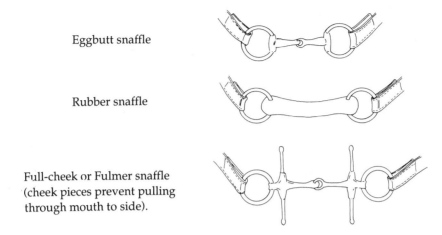

Snaffles *work on direct pressure principle: the amount of pressure the rider puts on the reins is the amount the*
horse feels.

FIGURE 9A: ***Some of the Most Common Kinds of Snaffle Bits***

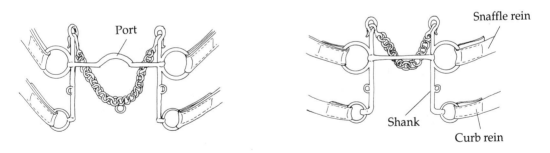

Port

Snaffle rein

Shank

Curb rein

A port allows space for the tongue, which increases the severity of the bit, as the tongue cannot cushion the impact
of the bit.

Snaffle reins: the amount of pressure the rider puts on the reins is the amount the horse feels.
Curb reins: the amount of pressure the rider puts on the reins is greatly magnified due to the long shank and the
curb chain, which tightens as the reins are pulled and exerts pressure under the chin at same time the crownpiece
of the bridle tightens on the horse's poll.

FIGURE 9B: ***Pelhams Work on Leverage Principle***

severity by allowing space for the horse's tongue, thus preventing the tongue from cushioning the horse's *bars* (the gums behind the incisors and before the molars where there are no teeth).

The *pelham* bit combines the functions of both snaffle and curb in one bit. There are two reins on each side of the bit, the upper of which is called the *snaffle rein* (not to be confused with a snaffle *bit*) and the lower rein of which is called the *curb rein*.

The snaffle rein is the milder of the two and works more or less as a regular snaffle bit would. Because the bit is not jointed and there is a lot more metal adding weight and movement to the bit, the snaffle rein of a curb bit cannot give as refined a signal as a snaffle bit alone would. The snaffle rein of a pelham bit should be held with very gentle contact or "feel" while riding. It should be used with more firmness only when the rider gives a particular aid.

The curb rein exerts leverage. It can cause real pain to the horse in the hands of an insensitive rider and must never be turned into an instrument of cruelty. The curb rein should normally remain slightly slack, and be used only in the event that the horse fails to respond to pressure on the snaffle rein. The curb rein tends to make the horse shorten his stride and slow down. Use it only enough to get the required action from the horse, and release any pressure or feel on it the instant the horse has responded.

A *full* or *double bridle*, consisting of two separate bits (a *bridoon*, or very thin snaffle, and a curb bit with chain), is not for use by the beginning rider; it is used only for specialized advanced work by an expert.

Most excellent riders generally use only a plain snaffle and school their horses to respond to it properly on light signals. This is vastly preferable to putting bits of greater and greater severity into a horse's mouth and relying on the pain they can induce to elicit obedience.

HOW TO PUT ON THE BRIDLE

First, give the horse a friendly pat on the neck and speak quietly to him so that he will feel confident that you mean him no harm. Have him in a stall or confined area so that he cannot walk away or on *cross ties*—that is, have him stand in a stall or hallway, attached to opposite walls by a rope and snap on each side of his *halter*. Be sure that he is clean and that his hair is smooth, as any roughness beneath the bridle will chafe (see *Grooming*, page 137). Place the reins over the horse's head and around his neck so that he will not step on them; this will also give you the means to hold onto him. Unbuckle the halter (see figure 10) on the left side, remove it, and hang it up. Never let any piece of tack fall on the ground, as it may get scraped or dirty or the horse may get tangled up in it.

Hold the left *cheekpiece* in your left hand, the right cheekpiece in your right hand. Facing the same direction as the horse, bring the cheekpieces up alongside the horse's head, one on either side of his head, until the bit just touches his lips. Do not force the bit into his mouth. Now transfer both cheekpieces into your right hand, forming a loose fist over the horse's nose about one-third of the way up it (see figure 11). Rest the bit on the thumb and second finger of your left hand, keeping the other fingers well out of the way (see figure 11). With your thumb, wiggle between his lips on the left side of the mouth at the bars. When the horse opens his mouth, raise the cheekpieces with your right hand and smoothly pull the bit into his

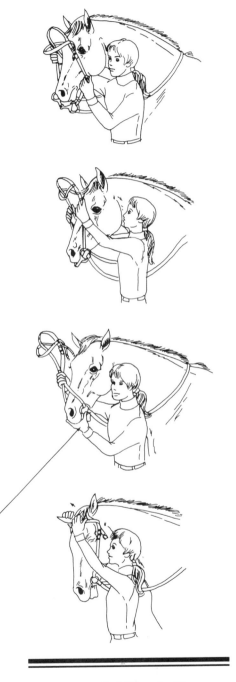

FIGURE 10:   *Bridling the Horse*

Standard halter, *made of double-stitched leather with brass fittings. Cheaper versions are made of nylon webbing with stainless steel fittings; however, these can be dangerous, as they do not break easily if a horse gets hung up in one.*

Grooming halter, *made of leather; easy to slip on and off. May have throatlatch with a snap (shown in dotted lines).*

FIGURE 11:   *Halters*

mouth. If he tries to raise his head, prevent this by holding his nose down with your right hand.

Reach under his jaw and up to his right ear with your left hand, point the ear into the hole formed by the *browband* and *crownpiece*, and gently poke it through. Do the same with the left ear. Smooth the forelock and pull it out from under the browband, and smooth the hair beneath the crownpiece with a finger. Fasten the *throatlatch* and the *cavesson* (or *noseband*).

Both cavesson and throatlatch should fit comfortably and loosely. In the case of the cavesson, you should be able to slip two or three fingers between it and the horse's jaw. With the throatlatch, a whole hand should fit easily between it and the horse's throat. Put all straps (those of the cheekpieces, the throatlatch, and the cavesson) into their *keepers* (small loops, like those on a belt, that prevent the loose end of a strap from flapping) so that no loose strap hits the horse's eye or face.

Be sure that the bit rests properly in the horse's mouth, neither too tightly nor too loosely (see figure 8, page 30). Bring the reins back over the horse's head and, when you prepare to put the saddle on, loop your left arm through them.

Never tie a horse by the reins; they break easily, and the bit may hurt the horse's mouth if he pulls back and breaks his bridle. A horse will quickly learn that bridles break whenever he runs back against them and may become quite professional about breaking them. If you must tie up a bridled horse, slip the halter on over the bridle and tie him up by the halter with a *lead shank* or cross ties, being sure that the reins rest on his neck so that he will not step on them.

The places where wear in the bridle is most likely to go undetected, and where it is therefore the most dangerous, are where the reins attach to the bit, where the cheekpieces attach to the bit, and where the cheekpieces attach to the crownpiece. No matter who put the bridle on the horse, it is of the utmost importance that you, the rider, check it over carefully. Once in the saddle, you will have only yourself to rely on if something goes wrong. A piece of leather that has not been correctly cared for can become cracked and dry, and can break. A broken rein or cheekpiece can cause an accident, one that is completely avoidable if you take the simple precaution of checking the tack before mounting any horse. Never trust that someone else has done this for you.

British-made bridles generally have better workmanship and leather than those made in other countries such as Argentina or India. Cheaper bridles are not necessarily bargains in the long run, and you will do better to invest in good quality from the beginning. Good tack, well cared for, will last a lifetime, while tack of inferior quality will fray, break, and wear out, requiring replacement within a short time regardless of how well you care for it.

When you remove the bridle, be sure to hold one hand on the horse's nose about one-third of the way up, to encourage him not to raise his head until he has spit out the bit. *If there is a curb chain, undo it first*, or the horse, unable to drop the bit, may raise his head and panic when the bit fails to come out of his mouth.

The Saddle

The *saddle* must fit the horse correctly so as not to injure his back. It must also fit the rider properly so as to place his or her weight in the correct position for balance, and in the best position to give the aids.

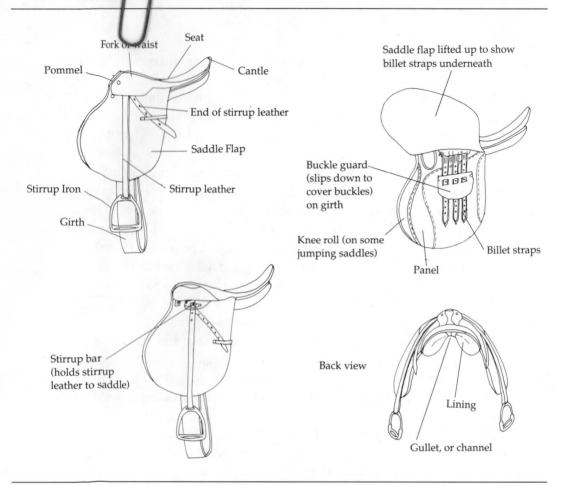

Fork or waist

Seat

Pommel

Cantle

End of stirrup leather

Saddle Flap

Stirrup Iron

Stirrup leather

Girth

Saddle flap lifted up to show
billet straps underneath

Buckle guard
(slips down to
cover buckles)
on girth

Knee roll (on some
jumping saddles)

Billet straps

Panel

Stirrup bar
(holds stirrup
leather to saddle)

Back view

Lining

Gullet, or channel

FIGURE 12:   *Parts of the Saddle*

The channel or *gullet* on the underside of the saddle (see figure 12) prevents the saddle from touching the horse's spine. The padding on either side of the gullet should be sufficient to allow you to "see daylight" when you look at the gullet from the front or back as it sits on the horse's back. If the saddle rests on the spine, serious damage can occur to the horse. In the same way, the padding under the front of the saddle should be sufficient so that the withers are protected. On a horse with very prominent withers, there is sometimes not enough room under the *pommel* to accommodate the extra height of the withers, which soon are rubbed raw. A *wither pad* (an oval knitted pad about twelve inches long by six inches wide, and one-quarter inch thick) is often placed between

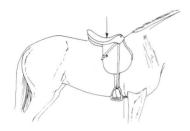

Correct: *Deepest part of seat is no farther than halfway back.*

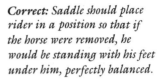

Correct: *Saddle should place rider in a position so that if the horse were removed, he would be standing with his feet under him, perfectly balanced.*

Incorrect: *Saddle places rider in a position so that if the horse were removed, he would fall backward.*

Incorrect: *Deepest part of seat is more than halfway back, throwing rider's weight too far back.*

FIGURE 13:   *How to Tell if a Saddle is Well Designed*

saddle and withers to provide extra padding. If this does not remedy the situation, a different saddle with either a higher pommel or a "cut-back" pommel must be used. On ponies with less prominent withers, a *crupper strap*, which fits under the dock and attaches to the saddle, may be necessary to prevent the saddle from slipping forward.

A *saddle pad* (or *numnah*) is made of felt, foam rubber, sheepskin, or a thick material resembling cotton terry cloth. Straps attach it from the front to the *billet straps* of the saddle. The saddle pad must be kept clean or it can chafe the horse's back. A pad made of washable material is therefore preferable to one of felt, which can only be brushed clean when dry and which tends to cake with sweat and dirt.

The most important feature of a well-designed saddle is that when it is in place on a horse and viewed from the side, the deepest point of the seat must not be farther back than the midpoint of the saddle (see figure 13). This is es-

A. Dressage Saddle

B. General Purpose Riding/
Jumping Saddle

C. Forward Seat Jumping Saddle with
padded knee rolls

FIGURE 14: *Types of Saddles*

sential, because it greatly affects how the rider sits on the horse. It is very difficult to sit in anyplace other than the seat's deepest point, and if this point is too far back the rider's entire balance will be thrown back. He or she will therefore be unable to give the aids effectively, or to move easily with the horse.

The seat of the saddle should be big enough for the rider to sit comfortably with about a hand's width of space in front and behind. A seat that is too large leaves the rider sliding around; one that is too small forces the rider to sit on the upward-slanted *cantle* and pommel. Seats, measured from the front of the pommel to the cantle, come in sizes ranging from children's (fourteen, fifteen, and sixteen inches for large and small ponies and all sizes of children) to adults' (from sixteen and one-half to eighteen or more inches in half-inch increments). Before buying one, it is best to try out several sizes—on a horse if possible, rather than on a sawhorse in a tack shop.

The *fork* or *waist* of the saddle should be narrow rather than flat and broad, as it is much easier to stay on a saddle with a narrow fork than on one with a flat, wide fork. The difference in stability is something like what you would feel sitting astride a narrow wall as opposed to sitting astride a round oil drum four feet in diameter.

Some jumping and general-purpose saddles have substantial padding both under and on the outside of the saddle flap. Called *knee rolls* (see figure 14c), these pads are sometimes covered in suede. Some riders like them, but others find the padding simply puts them farther from the horse. Extra padding may initially feel comfortable to a beginning rider, since it tends to relieve some of the unaccustomed strain on the muscles of the inner thigh. But anyone who really wants to develop a good seat is better advised to develop his or her muscles gradually on a saddle without extra padding from the start. There is a case to be made for the theory that "the less padding, the closer to the horse, and therefore the better."

It is far better to borrow a good saddle to learn on than to buy a badly designed one. Beginning riders, in their eagerness to own all their own equipment, often buy inferior saddles, but later find them difficult to sell, and are therefore unable to purchase the right ones. There may be exceptions, but in general, saddles made in India and Argentina use leather of quality inferior to British-made ones, and often their design is wrong for the British and American styles of riding, placing the rider too far back on the seat.

The costs of a good saddle, girth, stirrup leathers, and irons may be intimidating, but one redeeming factor in this high initial cost is that you can usually sell a good used saddle for almost as much as you paid for it (keeping in mind, however, that the cost of a new one increases every year).

If you do not want to invest too much initially, ask a Pony Club or a local riding stable if anyone has a good used saddle for sale. Sometimes you can find a bargain in a saddle that a child has outgrown, or a saddle for sale because its owner is leaving for college.

THE GIRTH

The *girth* must be kept free of sweat and dirt, as it can chafe the horse. There are various kinds (see figure 15). Perhaps the best is the elastic-end contour leather girth, which avoids chafing by its shape and is easy for the rider to *do up*, or fasten. In addition, it expands whenever necessary for the horse's comfort.

It is imperative to check both ends of the girth for signs of fraying elastic or stitching that has pulled out or become rotten. You must also check the sewing attaching the billet straps to the saddle, as well as the stitching on the stirrup leathers. If any of these should break you could have a dangerous fall, and this can be easily avoided by performing a simple check prior to mounting. Never depend on anyone else to do this for you.

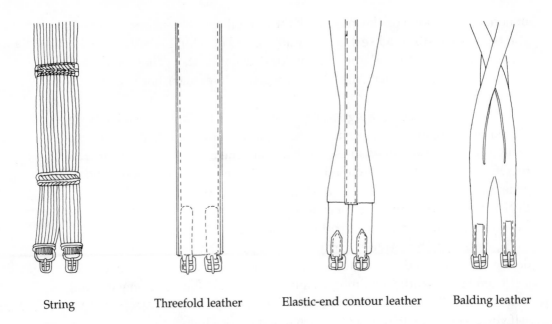

String

Threefold leather

Elastic-end contour leather

Balding leather

String: allows for air to circulate—strings roll rather than chafe.

Threefold leather: open fold goes toward rear of horse so as to not chafe elbows.

Elastic-end contour leather: elastic ends make doing up easier, and the elastic expands when required during work; cut at elbows so as not to chafe.

Balding leather: contour at elbows prevents chafing.

FIGURE 15:   *Types of Girth*

STIRRUPS

Stirrup irons hang from the saddle on *stirrup leathers*—straps about one inch wide and one to two and one-half feet long, with a buckle at one end. The end fits through a keeper on the saddle flap. The stirrup irons must be wide enough so that there is one-quarter to one-half inch on each side of the rider's foot when in the stirrup with the widest part of the foot on the hindmost edge of the stirrup (see figure 16). Never ride with stirrups narrower than this. If you should fall, your foot could become wedged in the iron, and you could be dragged by a panicking horse. The heavier the stirrups are, the better. Those with extra-thick *stirrup pads* (footrests) are best, because if you accidentally drop them, they fall straight down (rather than fly around as the lighter ones may) and are therefore easier to quickly regain.

HOW TO PUT ON THE SADDLE

FRONT VIEW
Incorrect: *No space between rider's foot and sides of stirrup—foot can get wedged in the stirrup iron.* ***Dangerous.*** ***Correct:*** *Stirrup allows ¼ inch on each side at widest part of rider's foot. Widest part of rider's foot (ball of foot) lies against the hindmost edge of the stirrup iron.*

BOTTOM VIEW
Incorrect: *No space*
Correct: *Space*

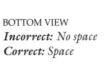

FIGURE 16: ***Stirrups***

Carry the saddle over your left arm with the pommel against your elbow and the stirrups *run up* (see figure 17). To do this, grasp the stirrup iron with your right hand and, with your left hand, take hold of the loop made by the leather near the bottom where it slips through the hole at the top of the iron. Slide the iron up the back side of the loop until it cannot go any higher. Tuck all the leathers through the part of the stirrup where your foot goes.

Lay the girth across the seat. Stand the saddle carefully on the ground against a wall, pommel down, with the girth between the cantle and the wall to prevent scraping the cantle.

To put on the saddle, first have the horse in a stall or confined area or on cross ties so that he cannot walk away, and have the bridle or a halter on him. Be sure that the horse is clean and that his hair lies smoothly. Run your hand over all the areas that the saddle will touch, including his back, girth area, and between and under his front legs. If there is any roughness, soreness, or swelling, do not saddle the horse, but have an expert look him over.

If the horse is bridled, loop the reins over your left arm, holding the saddle by the pommel in your left hand and the cantle in your right hand. Face the horse's left side. Place the girth, which should be attached by one end on the right (off) side of the saddle, across the seat of the saddle. Make sure that

1. *Hold the leather near the bottom with your left hand, grasp the iron with your right.*

2. *Slide the iron up the back side of the loop made by the leather until it cannot go any higher (you will hear the stirrup clink against the metal bar that holds it to the saddle).*

3. *Tuck all the leathers through the stirrup where your foot would go.*

FIGURE 17:   ***Running Up Stirrup Irons***

the stirrup irons are run up.

Place the saddle a few inches ahead of where it actually belongs on the horse's back, that is, with the pommel a little in front of the withers. If you are using a saddle pad you can either place the pad on first by itself, or place it on attached to the saddle. In either case, slide the saddle and/or pad backward so as to smooth the hair in the right direction (see figure 18). Be sure the pad is attached by its own straps to the billet straps under the saddle flap (check this before you do up the girth). If you are using a standing martingale, this must be slipped around the girth before you do it up.

When the saddle is moved smoothly into place with the pommel just behind the withers, walk around the front of the horse to the *off* (right) side and lift the girth down from the seat of the saddle, letting it hang straight down. Keep the reins looped over your arm while you do this. Lift the *saddle flap* to check for twisting and to see that the girth is buckled on evenly on the off side. Attach the girth by the front billet strap and either the middle or rear billet strap, allowing the unused strap to lie flat. If there is a *buckle guard*, put it down over the buckles so as to protect the underside of the saddle flap.

With the reins still looped over your left arm, return to the *near* (left) side of the horse and buckle the girth fairly loosely, using the two billet straps corresponding to those on the off side. Make no attempt to do up the girth tightly—the horse will guard against the sudden discomfort of a too-tight girth by expanding his lungs with air so that the girth will loosen when he exhales. Under no circumstances should you jab a horse's belly with a knee or elbow to make him expel the air; he will

Loop the reins over your left arm. Face the horse's left side. Place the saddle on the horse's back with the stirrups run up and the girth attached on the right side and lying across the seat of the saddle.

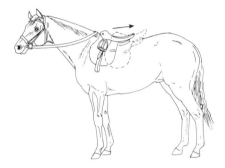

Place the saddle a few inches to the front of its proper place (solid line) then move it back until it is in the correct position on the horse's back (dotted lines).

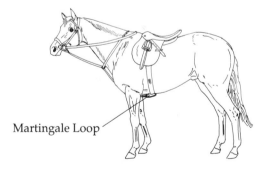

Martingale Loop

Check under the saddle flaps to be sure that the girth lies flat on both sides of the saddle. Do up the girth just tightly enough so that the saddle will stay on. (If there is a standing martingale, slip the girth through the lower loop end before doing up the girth.) Leave the stirrups up until just prior to mounting. Do up the girth a second time, snuggly, just before you mount, and after you have mounted and walked for a few minutes, tighten a third and final time.

FIGURE 18: ***Putting on the Saddle***

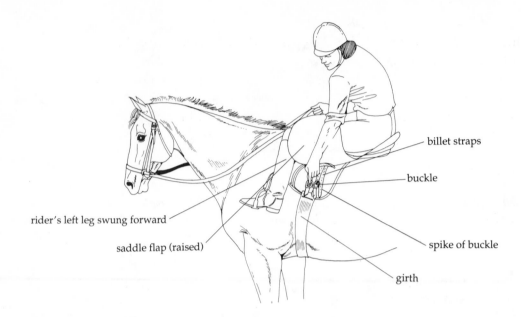

billet straps

buckle

rider's left leg swung forward

spike of buckle

saddle flap (raised)

girth

1. *Swing the left leg forward in front of the saddle flap, keeping your foot in the stirrup.*
2. *Lift up the saddle flap and hold in place with left arm.*
3. *Lay your left index finger against the buckled billet strap. Pick up the end of the strap and hold across the left palm of your hand.*

4. *Pull up, on the billet strap.*
5. *Push the spike of the buckle into the new hole and smooth down the billet straps; slide down the buckle guard.*
6. *Replace the saddle flap, resume position in saddle.*

FIGURE 19:   ***Tightening the Girth While Mounted***

soon dread the sight of both the saddle and you. Instead, merely make a practice of doing up the girth just tightly enough to keep it initially in place; then lead the horse a few yards or more away, by which time you will be easily able to pull up the girth again just prior to mounting. Tighten it a third and final time when you are in the saddle (see figure 19), as your weight will cause the saddle to settle downward and the girth to loosen.

Before you remove the saddle, first loosen the girth for a few minutes. This is especially important in winter, as the horse's back may become damp, causing the blood vessels in the area where the saddle rests to expand; a sudden draft of cold air can give a horse in this condition a sore back.

Next undo the billet straps. If the horse is wearing a standing martingale be certain to slip the martingale off the girth as soon as you undo the billet straps.

Otherwise the saddle can fall off the horse while remaining attached by the martingale and cause the horse to panic.

Always *lift* the saddle off the horse's back. Do not pull the saddle sideways, as this could bruise the horse's withers.

In cold or windy weather place a horse blanket over the horse's back after you've removed the saddle.

The Standing Martingale

The *standing martingale* is composed of two straps of leather. The first strap is about an inch wide, with a small, stitched loop that attaches to the noseband at one end and a larger, buckled loop that attaches to the girth at the other (see figure 20). The standing mar-

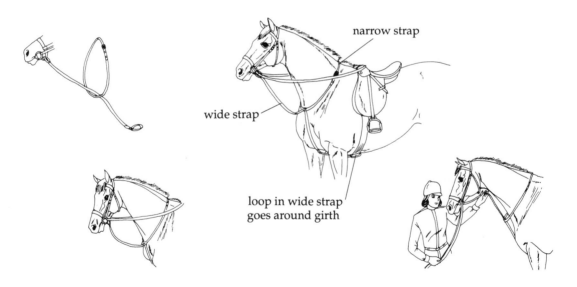

narrow strap

wide strap

loop in wide strap
goes around girth

The Standing Martingale prevents the horse from raising his head too high to be controllable by the rider. To measure proper adjustment of martingale, push it upward (lower right). It should just reach the throat when

FIGURE 20:   *The Standing Martingale*

tingale can be used only with an ordinary noseband, never with a *dropped nose-band* (one that fits snugly just behind the horse's chin to prevent his opening his mouth). The combination of a standing martingale and a dropped nose-band would impede the horse's breathing. A second strap, about one-half inch wide, goes around the base of the horse's neck and, by means of a small slot, holds the first strap in place. The second strap is adjusted by means of a small buckle that goes on the near (left) side of the horse's neck.

The function of a standing martingale is to prevent the horse from raising his head above a certain point. It is adjustable by means of a large buckle between the horse's front legs at the girth. When properly adjusted, a standing martin-gale exerts no pressure on the noseband unless the horse raises his head to an unnaturally high position (usually to avoid obeying a signal that the rider has given). The martingale is correctly adjusted if it just meets the horse's throat when you push it upward with your hand.

HOW TO PUT ON THE STANDING MARTINGALE

Have the horse bridled and saddled with the girth attached on the off (right) side only, and hanging down straight. Place the narrow strap of the martingale, buckled to form a large loop, around the horse's neck so that the buckle is on the near (left) side of the neck, leaving the wider strap hanging down freely. Undo the noseband. Grasp the end of the wider strap, which has a small stitched loop at one end about two inches in diameter. Pass the end of the nose-band through this loop and rebuckle the noseband. Take the other end of the same strap and pass the girth through the loop with the buckle, being sure that the buckle faces downward so its spike does not irritate the horse's skin. The strap should be centrally positioned where it meets the girth, and not slid over to one side.

After doing up the girth loosely, test the length of the martingale strap with your hand by pushing the strap upward toward the horse's throat. If the strap just meets his throat when his head is in a relaxed position, it is properly ad-justed. If there is pressure on it when his head is in a relaxed position, it is too tight. If it fails to prevent his head from being raised above a normal position, it is too loose. Make the necessary adjustments at the buckle end located at the girth.

The Whip

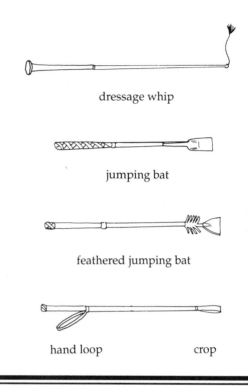

dressage whip

jumping bat

feathered jumping bat

hand loop   crop

FIGURE 21: *Types of Whips*

A *riding whip* should be carried every time you ride (see figure 21). At some time, even the best-behaved horse will refuse to go forward, and this can lead to serious vices if not corrected at once. Carrying a whip will become second nature to you and you should quickly be able to carry it in either hand with equal ease.

A *crop* is a thin whip about two feet long with a narrow leather tab at one end and a thin wrist strap at the other. Crops tend to be flimsy and too thin to be comfortably held. They are generally covered with inexpensive leather and fall apart quickly.

A *jumping bat* is similar to a crop, but is much sturdier and usually a little shorter. It can be either plain or "feathered" (with small leather pieces sticking out along a part of its length below the handle). A bat should have a fiberglass core, which provides the right "feel" and stiffness, covered in leather or good quality synthetic materials (which resemble leather and sometimes last longer), and a good, large, stiff "popper" (leather tab) on its end. Its handle should be thick enough to be held in the hand easily. Very thin-handled whips are tiring to the hand and should be avoided.

The *dressage whip*, which is nearly twice as long as a jumping bat, has a fiberglass core covered with densely woven threads. It has a large, flat head that prevents its slipping through your hand. It has the advantage of being easy to use while you keep your hand on the rein.

Any whip must be long enough to reach easily across your knee when your hands are on the reins, with five or six inches on the lower end and two to four inches extending above your hand on the reins. Avoid any whip that is overly pliable or "rubbery," because you will not be able to apply a solidly placed tap with it.

QUIZ

1. Which of the following items are included under the heading of *tack*?
   (A) saddle   (B) whip
   (C) horseshoes (D) bridle
   (E) martingale
   (F) brushes and currycombs

2. *True or false:* As soon as you begin to learn to ride, you should purchase your own tack.

3. The mildest bit of the following is a
   (A) curb bit   (B) snaffle bit
   (C) curb bit with a port mouth

4. Another name for the noseband of a bridle is a
   (A) headstall   (B) crownpiece
   (C) cavesson

5. A port in a curb bit makes the bit
   (A) more severe   (B) less severe

6. The curb bit works on the principle of
   (A) pressure and leverage
   (B) direct action

7. Which bit uses double reins?
   (A) curb bit   (B) snaffle bit

8. On a bit with double reins, which rein should remain slightly slack except when needed?
   (A) curb rein   (B) snaffle rein

9. Which of the following is *not* part of a plain snaffle bridle?
   (A) crownpiece   (B) cheekpiece
   (C) browband
   (D) cavesson or noseband
   (E) egg butt bit   (F) throatlatch
   (G) bridoon   (H) laced reins

10. *True or false:* A snaffle bit is properly adjusted when it just wrinkles the corners of the horse's mouth.

11. *True or false:* When saddling your horse, it is a good idea to bridle him first so you can tie him up by the reins as you saddle him.

12. The places where wear in the bridle is most likely to go undetected and is therefore most dangerous are
    (A) where the reins buckle together near where the rider holds them
    (B) where the reins attach to the bit
    (C) where the cheekpieces attach to the bit
    (D) where the cheekpieces attach to the crownpiece

13. *True or false:* In general, saddles made in England are superior to those made in other countries.

14. The straps that hold the girth to the saddle are called
    (A) girth guards   (B) billets
    (C) leathers

15. Which gives the rider more security on a saddle?
    (A) a narrow fork (B) a wide fork

16. When saddling a horse, you should place the saddle
    (A) a little in front of where it belongs and slide it back
    (B) a little behind where it belongs and slide it forward
    (C) exactly where it belongs

17. With what kind of cavesson or noseband should you *never* use a standing martingale?
    (A) double stitched   (B) dropped
    (C) ordinary

18. Which way should the spike on the buckle of a standing martingale point?
    (A) toward the horse
    (B) away from the horse

19. A standing martingale is properly adjusted when the wider strap that runs from the cavesson to the girth
    (A) just meets the throat of the horse when you push it upward with your hand
    (B) is equal in length to the narrower band that goes around the horse's neck
    (C) pulls the horse's head down slightly when he carries it in a normal position

20. When should you carry a whip?
    (A) only on balky horses, never on skittish ones
    (B) every time you ride *any* horse
    (C) only when riding in a ring or enclosed area

21. When should a beginning rider wear spurs?
    (A) only while riding under supervision
    (B) only on very sluggish horses
    (C) not until his or her leg position is absolutely steady and an instructor advises that he or she is ready to do so

5

How Do Horses Think and Act?

A HORSE is not a machine. Every horse is a living, breathing creature with feelings, emotions, likes and dislikes, and a distinct personality all his own. Some are naturally outgoing, others shy; some are bossy; some are busybodies; a certain few possess a demonstrable sense of humor. Horses have days when they feel cheerful, and days when they feel out of sorts and probably would just prefer to be left alone.

One inborn characteristic all horses share lies beneath the surface at all times: the instinct to look for and run from danger. This instinct can no more be trained out of a horse than a person can train himself not to blink when someone else makes a sudden movement toward his or her eyes. Over millions of years, the only horses who survived to breed were those with a healthy fear of danger and the speed to run from it; slow or incautious horses got eaten by predators. Consequently, this instinct is at the very core of every horse's nature. Understanding this will let a beginning rider take the first step toward learning to "think like a horse" and thereby anticipate and correct potential prob-

As he approaches a fence, the horse lowers and extends his head and neck prior to take-off in order to focus on the take-off point.

FIGURE 22:   ***Approaching a Fence***

lems while riding rather than simply battle against instinctive behavior.

The principal ways a horse looks for danger are through the senses of sight, hearing, and smell. A horse's sight is different from a person's in that his eye does not focus by means of a lens that changes shape; rather, he moves his whole head in such a way that the retina, where the optic nerve endings are located at the back of the eye, receives light at the spots where it provides the clearest picture. You can observe this head movement while riding across country or as a horse approaches a fence he must jump. While riding across a field, a horse constantly lifts and lowers his head to get a better view of distant objects, and as he approaches a fence he must jump, he extends and lowers his head on the last two or three strides in order to precisely judge his moment of takeoff (see figure 22).

Unlike a person's eyes, a horse's eyes are located on opposite sides of his head rather than in the front. Each eye sees an entirely different view on its own side of the head. A horse's vision is therefore panoramic; he can look ahead and behind at the same moment. However, because his vision is not binocular (both eyes focusing on the same object simultaneously), a horse lacks a three-dimensional picture and accurate depth perception.

A horse's hearing is many times more acute than a person's. His ears, which can turn more than 180 degrees, funnel sound with great efficiency. In addition, a horse can sense sounds at a great distance—sometimes a mile or more away—by vibrations transmitted through his hooves on the ground.

His sense of smell is also acute, and when he perceives danger nearby, the horse makes every effort to inhale as much of the smell as possible to try to figure out what it is and how near it is. When he exhales all the air he has taken

in, he makes the loud snorting noise characteristic of a frightened horse (not to be confused with the rapid flapping noises of sneezing, or with those of *high-blowing*, heard at the gallop, in which exhalation is so forceful and fast that the soft skin of the nostril vibrates).

Herd instinct is strong, because in case of danger any member of the group can alert the others, and several sets of eyes, ears, and noses have a better chance of spotting danger than does a lone horse. For this reason most horses are uneasy when being ridden alone across country, and you seldom see a horse grazing alone by choice. If horses are lying down to rest in a field, one usually remains standing, watching for danger.

Within a group of horses, a distinct "pecking order" is quickly established. Over millions of years, herds with weak or stupid leaders did not survive, so the herd's leader is usually the smartest and strongest horse—frequently a mare, not a stallion—or sometimes a less physically strong but aggressive horse who is smart enough to convince the others that he or she is stronger than they are. Once the pecking order is established, there is usually no fighting among herd members unless a new horse is introduced into the group. Then the newcomer must find his place within the group. The top horse may threaten to kick or bite any of the others, the number two horse may kick or bite any in the group except the top horse, and so on down to the bottom horse, who does not get to pick on anybody and has to stay out of the way of everybody.

Horses have, for each generation over the past several million years, spent nearly all their waking hours walking slowly, searching out and nibbling at grasses. Their circulation is geared to constant, very slow motion, and so is their digestive process. (This is one reason that horses with broken legs so often cannot be saved; the leg itself would mend in time, but meanwhile circulatory complications would develop due to enforced lack of movement.) During grazing, mucus runs downward and out of the nostrils so that dust and particles that would irritate sensitive membranes are not able to enter the nose. For millions of generations, the only reason a horse broke into a canter or gallop or jumped anything was to avoid life-threatening danger. Once safe, he returned to his normal routine of nibbling and walking slowly, hour after hour, every day of his life.

Today, we make demands of the horse in addition to the burden we put on his back. We expect a horse to walk, trot, canter, and jump on command, every time we ask him to, without argument or resistance.

We feed at specific times during the day—times that are convenient for people, but unnatural for horses whose digestive systems are designed to require the constant, slow intake of unconcentrated food, like grasses and small leafy plants. Long ago, in the natural state, the only grains a horse ate were the sparse seeds nibbled from the tops of wild grasses. Now we feed him buckets of highly concentrated grains and sweet feeds and rich grasses like alfalfa hay. So it should not surprise us that a horse who discovers an unattended feed bin eats all he can. He is simply following his instinct to eat as much as possible for as long as possible. He has no way of knowing that the rich concentrations of this food that human beings have chosen for him can kill him in large doses.

Unknowledgeable owners place a horse's hay high up in a hayrack; this keeps it off the ground where the horse could trample it, but it also puts it at a level where dust and irritating particles drop directly into the horse's sensitive nasal passages. A horse develops respiratory ailments when enough dust enters nasal passages never meant to be exposed to irritants. This is aggravated by work that is too strenuous for damaged lungs and air passages. So the small blood vessels of the lungs break down, causing *heaves*, a persistent cough, and the inability to do fast or strenuous work thereafter.

Unthinking people expect a horse to remain cooped up twenty-three hours a day in a space barely large enough for him to turn around in, then come out and work for an hour with a calm and obedient attitude. A horse needs to be turned out every day to graze, roll, play, express various aspects of his instinct as a member of a herd (including biting and kicking), and simply walk around where he pleases. If we prevent these natural actions, we prevent the expression of instinctive behavior. A horse interfered with in this way will attempt to carry out these instinctive urges while being ridden. Ignorant riders then wonder why their horses buck, kick, attempt to shy at everything in sight, or try to roll while being ridden.

Horses develop psychological problems—tense, angry, or explosive "hyper" personalities—due to improper handling and riding or to excessive confinement. They develop self-destructive habits from boredom, like *cribbing* (sucking air while biting down on a fence or doortop) and *weaving* (moving monotonously back and forth from one forefoot to the other). They can develop physical ailments like lameness from fast work on hard surfaces. (Keep in mind that anything faster than a walk is "fast" from the standpoint of a horse's evolution.) Almost everything a horse becomes that differs from the calm, gentle animal who is alert for danger, but at peace with his world, can be traced directly to mistakes made by human beings.

The intelligent rider adapts his or her methods of training and caring for a horse so that these adverse effects are minimized. The well-treated horse who is allowed to graze in a pasture for most (or all) of the day and night is happier than one confined and mistreated and then punished for simply reacting like a horse.

Horses never forget. Once a horse has learned a response, whether good or bad from the rider's point of view, he will remember it and prefer to always respond in the same way. For this reason, it is essential to handle and ride every horse correctly from the very beginning. Although a horse can be trained to unlearn a bad response (for instance, running back to the barn at the end of a ride), he will never entirely forget that that response worked well the first time and he may attempt to repeat it when the opportunity presents itself.

A horse does not magically know that a rider is a beginner and therefore decide to take advantage of the situation. Rather, he begins to respond in the old, undesirable way. For instance, if a horse begins to increase his pace on the way home from a ride, an experienced rider will feel him take the *first* step that is too fast, and will check his speed instantly, repeating this correction as often as the horse attempts to increase his speed to the slightest degree. But a beginning rider may not recognize the first moment that the increase in speed occurs; he or she will fail to check it until the horse has picked up considerable momentum and the problem has become much more difficult to correct.

A horse always attempts to act out the instinctive behavior of his species. A good rider simply *limits the horse's options, making all undesired responses uncomfortable or unpleasant enough so the horse chooses the only response left, that which the rider intends.* With correct riding, it becomes less and less often necessary to enforce the rules, as a horse quickly learns that it is in his own best interests to do what you ask for in the first place, since you will immediately cease giving the signal (*aid*) when he responds, but keep insisting if he does not.

Therefore, it is crucial that as a beginning rider you learn both *what* the aids are and *how* to give them—the "language" with which you communicate with a horse. You should learn these aids and their applications under controlled conditions—under the instruction of an expert teacher—where the chances of the horse's doing something you are not yet ready to correct are minimized. You must never be placed in a situation where you do not yet know how to deal with what the horse may do. There is absolutely nothing to be gained by the "sink or swim" method, and a great deal of harm, both physical and psychological, can result to both horse and rider.

QUIZ

1. The one inborn characteristic that all horses share is the
   (A) instinctive need to jump over small obstacles
   (B) instinctive need to buck and rear
   (C) instinct to look for and run from danger

2. Regarding a horse's vision, which of the following statements are true?
   (A) A horse's eye does not focus by means of a lens that changes shape.
   (B) A horse's vision is binocular (both eyes focus on the same object at the same time).
   (C) A horse focuses on an object by moving his whole head until the retina receives light where it provides him the clearest picture.
   (D) A horse can see ahead of and behind himself at the same moment.

3. *True or false:* A horse's ears can turn 180 degrees.

4. *High-blowing* is a sound made by a horse who is
   (A) very frightened
   (B) out of breath (or with broken wind)
   (C) exhaling forcefully at the gallop

5. Horses prefer to graze
   (A) in a group
   (B) alone, except when forced to join others in a small area
   (C) during the summer

6. A horse's circulation and digestion are, by evolution, suited to
   (A) slow, constant motion and nibbling of foods of low concentration
   (B) fast work on hard ground
   (C) several meals daily of highly concentrated foods like alfalfa and nutritious grains

7. In the stable, it is best to place a horse's hay
   (A) on the ground, even though he may step on it
   (B) in a hayrack five or six feet above the ground where there is no chance he will step on it

8. Biting down on a stall door or fence top while inhaling air is called
   (A) foundering
   (B) weaving
   (C) cribbing

9. *True or false:* The "sink of swim" method is a good way to learn to ride, as it forces the rider to learn quickly.

10. *True or false:* Horses quickly forget what they have experienced, whether it is good or bad.

Answers: 1C, 2A,C,D, 3. true, 4C, 5A, 6A, 7A, 8C, 9. false, 10. false

6

Mounting and Dismounting; Falls

Mounting

There are several different ways of mounting and dismounting, each with advantages and disadvantages. You should learn them all and use whichever is best in a given situation.

The horse should be led out with the reins brought over his head (see figure 23). Hold the buckle of the reins in your left hand and the reins about six to ten inches below the bit in your right hand for leading. Never attempt to lead a horse without taking the reins in this manner, because he could suddenly pull back and you would have no way of preventing his breaking away. The stirrups should be run up (see figure 17, page 42). Always check your tack before you mount any horse. Lift the saddle flap (skirt) on each side and check the girth; be sure that the stitching is in good repair at the girth ends at the buckles. Check the billet straps where they attach to the saddle for loose or rotted stitching. If the billet straps pull loose, the saddle can fall off while you are riding. The girth should be fairly loosely done up for the time being, just tight enough to hold the saddle in place. Just before

Incorrect: If reins are left over the horse's neck, the horse can pull backward and break free.

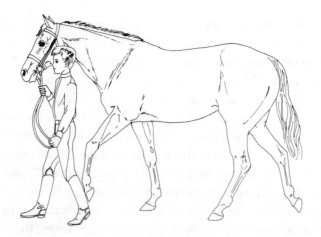

Correct: Reins are brought over the horse's head. Right hand holds reins a few inches below bit, left hand holds reins at the buckle.

FIGURE 23:   *Leading*

mounting, pull the girth up snugly enough so the saddle will not turn from side to side, and tighten it a third time after you are mounted, or have ridden for a few minutes.

If there is a martingale, see that it is properly adjusted (see figure 20) and that the buckle spike is pointed away from, not toward, the horse's skin. See that the saddle pad lies smoothly and that it is attached to the billet straps by its own straps at the front.

Check that the bridle is properly adjusted so that the bit barely wrinkles the corners of the horse's mouth. If you are using a pelham bit, be sure that the curb chain is not twisted and lies smoothly. All straps must be in their keepers. Check for signs of weakness in the leather where the cheekpieces attach to the bit, where the reins attach to the bit, and where the cheekpieces attach to the crownpiece. Be sure that the throatlatch is not too tight.

No matter who has tacked up a horse for you, it is your own responsibility to check over the tack before mounting. If a piece of tack breaks while you are riding, it is you who will pay the price of an accident regardless of whose fault it was for using unsafe tack or adjusting it improperly.

PREPARING TO MOUNT

Pull up the girth on the near (left) side of the horse. It should be as tight as you can conveniently adjust it just prior to mounting so that the saddle will not turn from side to side as you mount. But do not pull it so tight that it is painful to the horse.

MOUNTING FROM THE GROUND

Pull down the stirrup irons. Adjust them to approximately the correct length before mounting by placing the knuckles of your left hand at the top of the leathers where they attach to the saddle and pulling down the bottom of the irons with your right hand, adjusting them so the stirrup extends the length of your outstretched arm (see figure 24). The ends of the leathers

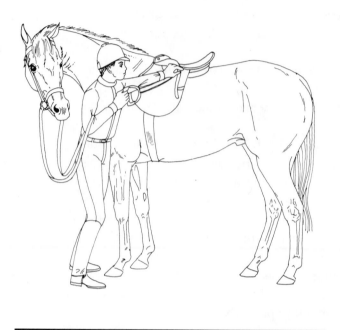

FIGURE 24:   *Adjusting the Stirrups to Approximate Length Before Mounting*

should hang free; do not put them into their keepers yet because you may have to adjust the stirrups further after you are in the saddle.

Place the reins on the horse's neck and put the buckle on his neck just in front of the withers. Stand on the left side of the horse, facing the shoulder, your whip in your left hand, hanging down. Do not put the whip in your right hand as it will wave around while you mount. Take the buckle of the reins with your right hand and draw it back until the reins are slightly taut, just enough so that the horse will not walk forward as you mount (see figure 25a). Now, with your left hand, grasp both reins and a handful of mane just in front of the withers. The reins, which you keep separated with one or two fingers, should be the same length, or alternatively the *off* (right) rein may be slightly shorter than the *near* (left) rein so that the horse will be discouraged from turning toward you when you put weight on the left stirrup to mount. Let the *bight*, the extra rein between your hand and the buckle, fall to the off (right) side of the horse.

Turn to face the horse's hip, with your left shoulder near his near (left) shoulder, as this enables you to regain your balance more easily if the horse takes a step. Holding the reins and mane with your left hand, take with your right hand the side of the stirrup that is located toward the rear of the horse. Place the tip of your left boot in the stirrup iron and push down on your toe as you press the left side of your knee against the saddle, in order to not jab the horse's side with your toe (see figure 25b). If the horse moves, hop forward or backward on your right foot as needed in order to keep your balance, but do not let go of the reins and mane with your left hand. At the beginning, until you can

A

Take the buckle of the reins in your right hand and draw it back so the reins are slightly taut. With your left hand, grasp both reins and a handful of mane just in front of the withers.

B

Put your left foot in the stirrup. Press your left knee against the saddle so as not to jab the horse's side with your toe.

C

Grasp the cantle or the waist of the saddle on the far side and spring upward. Divide your weight so that half is on the stirrup and the other half is divided equally between your left and right hands.

D

Swing your right leg over the croup as you transfer your right hand to the pommel or knee roll.

E

Take up the reins.

FIGURE 25:   ***Mounting from the Ground***

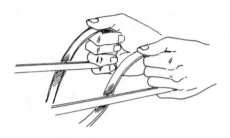

Position of hands when holding snaffle (single) reins.

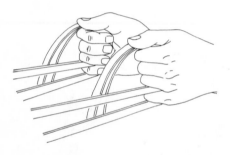

Position of hands when holding reins of pelham bit (double reins).

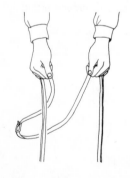

FIGURES 26, 27, 28: *Holding the Reins*

easily mount, your instructor should hold onto the bridle and off (right) stirrup to prevent the horse from moving.

Bend your right leg slightly in order to be able to spring upward, grasp either the cantle or the waist of the saddle on the off (right) side with your right hand, bounce two or three times on your right foot, and spring upward. Your right hand gripping the saddle and your left hand on the mane will help to pull you upward.

When you are standing above the horse, with your left foot in the left stirrup, and facing the horse with your weight on the ball of your foot, divide your weight so that half is on the stirrup and the other half is supported equally by your left and right hands (see figure 25c).

Keeping your right leg fairly straight, swing it over the horse's croup, being careful not to touch the horse. At the same time, transfer your right hand from the cantle or the waist of the saddle to the pommel or to the right knee roll (see figure 25d). Gently lower yourself into the saddle and take up the reins (see figure 25e). Never let your weight fall heavily or suddenly onto the horse's back. Any horse jolted in this manner will protest—justifiably—and his resulting vices will be difficult to correct; most commonly, the horse will move off at a trot or even gallop before you have completed mounting.

Take up your reins quietly (see figure 26). If you are using a snaffle bit, there will be a single rein on each side of the horse's neck. The rein should pass from the horse's mouth between your ring finger and your little finger, cross your palm, and come out the top of your loosely curled fingers. Your thumb lies on top and goes in the same direction as

Incorrect: Arms and reins do not form a straight line from elbow to bit when seen from above.

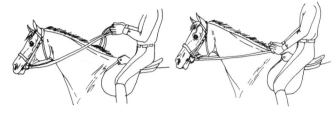

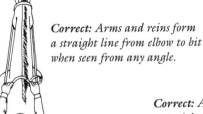

Correct: Arms and reins form a straight line from elbow to bit when seen from any angle.

Incorrect: Arms and reins do not form a straight line from elbow to bit when seen from side view.

Correct: Arms and reins form a straight line from elbow to bit when seen from side view.

FIGURE 29: *Holding the Reins*

the rein; in the event that the horse pulls the rein, downward pressure from your thumb will prevent the reins from slipping through your hand. The *bight* (extra rein) should fall between your two hands on the off side of the horse.

If you are using a pelham bit, there will be two reins on each side of the horse's neck, a snaffle rein and a curb rein. The snaffle rein goes exactly where it does with a snaffle bit. The curb rein, which must be held slightly slack (except when it is being actively used), passes from the horse's mouth to the outside of your hand beneath your little finger. Both reins then lie flat together, across your palm, and come out the top of your hand together, held in place by your thumb (see figure 27).

Your hands should be held with the thumbs uppermost and the knuckles pointing forward and slightly inward (see figure 28). You can tilt both hands very slightly inward, but do not turn them so far that they become flat, with the backs uppermost. Your wrists should have no bend in them, but should be held on the same straight plane as your lower arm. The object is to form the shortest distance, a straight line, from elbow to bit via your arm and the reins when seen from any angle. Any bend in the wrist or hand that interrupts this straight line adds unnecessary distance between the bit and your hand (see figure 29). The communication between your hands and the horse's mouth is called *contact*.

SHORTENING THE REINS

Your hands must remain in front of the horse's withers in order to be well placed to give signals (aids) to the horse. If the reins are too long, shorten them by one of the following two methods:

While riding at the walk, trot, or canter, reach across with the thumb and forefinger of your right hand and grasp the left rein where it falls free—*not*, that is, the part between your left hand and the bit, but rather close behind the hand, where the rein hangs loosely down (the *bight*). Slide your left hand forward, but maintain equal pressure on both reins as you do so. Repeat on the right side, using your left hand to maintain pressure as you shorten your right rein.

Horses tend to move faster as you shorten the reins because they associate shortening with being asked to trot or canter, which requires shorter reins, or with being tapped with the whip, which requires the rider to first transfer the reins to one hand. So with most horses you must maintain slight pressure on both reins as you shorten them to counteract this tendency to move faster.

A second method of shortening the reins can be used if you are holding the reins by the buckle in *free walk* (when there is no contact at all with the horse's mouth, and he is encouraged to extend his head and neck in a restful position). To shorten the reins quickly in such a situation, grasp the buckle in one hand, clasp the other hand loosely around the reins above the withers, and pull back on the first hand, exactly as you would to shorten the reins prior to mounting.

Once mounted, take up your right stirrup by turning your toe inward and moving your foot about until the ball of your foot lies squarely across the bottom of the iron.

ADJUSTING THE LENGTH OF THE STIRRUPS WHILE MOUNTED

A rough guide for judging the proper length of the stirrups is to remove your foot from the stirrup and let your leg fall as long as is comfortable. When the bottom of the stirrup hits your ankle bone in this position, the stirrup is approximately the right length for general riding.

• *To shorten the right stirrup:* Hold both reins with your left hand. Bring your right leg back. Lighten the downward pressure on the stirrup, grasp the end of the stirrup leather above the buckle, and pull the strap upward, keeping your

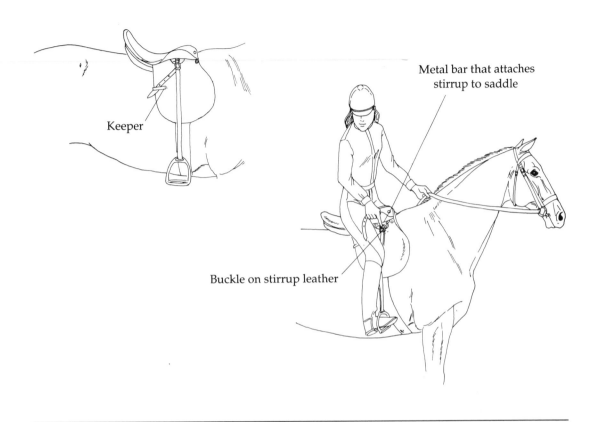

Keeper

Metal bar that attaches
stirrup to saddle

Buckle on stirrup leather

FIGURE 30:   *Adjusting the Stirrups While Mounted*

index finger on the spike of the buckle. When the desired hole is reached, push
the spike into the hole with your index finger. Be sure to slide the buckle back as
far as it will go, so that the top of the buckle clicks against the metal bar that
holds it to the saddle. Place the end of the stirrup leather in its keeper (see
figure 30).

• *To lengthen the right stirrup:* Repeat the above process, but push *down* with
your foot until the proper length has been reached.

MOUNTING WITH A MOUNTING BLOCK

In order to use a *mounting block* (a block usually about one to one and one-
half feet high, and wide enough to stand on comfortably), lead the horse by the

reins brought out over his head. Keeping the block on his near (left) side, make him stand as close as possible alongside the mounting block. Check your tack, pull down the stirrup irons, and mount as you would if mounting from the ground.

However, unless a rider is elderly or disabled, or the horse is extremely large (in which case he is probably too big for the rider), the beginner should learn to mount without the aid of a mounting block. Anyone who comes to rely on its use may be unable to remount if he or she comes off the horse when the mounting block is not nearby.

MOUNTING FROM THE WRONG (OFF) SIDE

To mount from the off side, follow the instructions for mounting from the ground, but in each case substitute left for right. A horse with no practice in this exercise may initially be uneasy. Have an assistant hold him in case he attempts to take a step in any direction.

Mounting from the wrong side is excellent practice, and it may stand you in good stead if you find yourself prevented by terrain from mounting from the near side; on a narrow ledge, for example, you may be unable to move to the usual side of the horse to mount. It feels quite awkward for most riders to mount from the off side until they have practiced it a good deal, but riders who learn to mount from either side from the start will never have any difficulty.

GETTING A "LEG UP"

Mounting with the assistance of another person who helps to lift you into the air high enough for you to swing your right leg over the horse's croup is called *getting a leg up* (see figure 31).

If you are mounting with the aid of a leg up, stand beside the horse, holding the reins and a handful of mane in your left hand as you would when mounting from the ground (see figure 25, page 63). With your right hand grasp the cantle of the saddle. Face the horse's side, and bend your left knee sharply so that your shin is parallel to the ground. Keep your knee bent for the entire time you are being assisted; otherwise it will be impossible for the assistant to lift you easily into the air. The person assisting should stand behind you and slightly to your left.

On a prearranged signal (usually on the count of *"three!"*) spring upward from your right foot. The assistant, holding you at the knee with his or her left hand and at the ankle with his or her right, lifts you quickly into the air, straight up, making no attempt to move you closer to the horse. You should assist this movement by pulling yourself up with your left hand on the mane (holding the reins) and your right hand on the cantle.

When you are high enough in the air, swing your right leg over the horse's croup, being careful not to touch the horse as you do so. At the same time, transfer your right hand to the right knee roll or to the pommel of the saddle and place as much weight as possible onto both hands.

Then lower yourself gently into the saddle, being careful not to fall heavily onto the horse's back. At this point the assistant releases your left leg. Take up your stirrups (by turning your toes inward

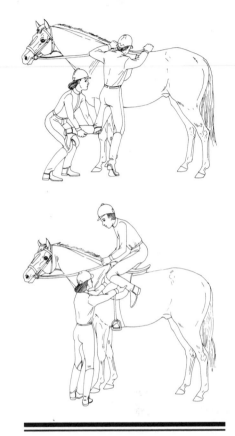

FIGURE 31: *Getting a "Leg Up"*

to pick up the stirrup irons where they lie flat against the horse's sides) and take up the reins in the regular way.

Every rider should know both how to give and how to get a leg up. It is a useful way of mounting a green (untrained) horse or a skittish one who will not stand quietly while you mount in the usual way.

MOUNTING BAREBACK

There are two ways to mount a horse bareback. Both work equally well on small horses and ponies; the second may work better on large horses. Any rea-

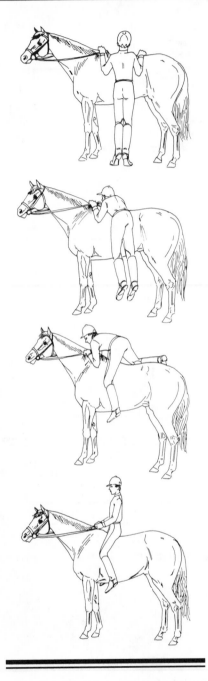

FIGURE 32A: *Mounting Bareback,*
First Method

sonably athletic person can, with practice, learn to mount horses of almost any size using the second method. Have someone hold the horse when you practice mounting bareback; it will take you several attempts to learn to do it smoothly.

• *The first method* (see figure 32a) entails facing the horse's side, holding the reins and mane with your left hand. Place your right hand, palm downward, on the horse's back at about the point where the cantle would be if the horse were saddled. Bend both knees, and spring upward and toward the horse, getting your belly across his back, sideways. Wriggle far enough across the horse's back to slide your right leg across the croup, sit upright, and take up the reins in the usual way.

• *The second method* of mounting bareback (see figure 32b) requires some practice, but, once learned, works well on almost any-size horse.

Hold the reins and a good handful of mane with your left hand, about eight inches in front of the withers. Turn your body so that your back is close to the horse's neck. In one swift movement, take a step toward the rear of the horse with your right foot followed immediately by one with your left foot, pushing off as you do so, and swinging your right foot into the air. Your left hand on the mane helps to pull you upward, and the momentum generated by the two quick steps allows you to swing upward. Grasp the withers with your right hand as you swing upward. Hook your right heel over the horse's back and pull yourself upright, taking up the reins in the usual way.

With both methods of mounting bareback, it is best to initially have an assistant hold the reins; any horse not accustomed to these methods may try to move as you practice.

FIGURE 32A: *Mounting Bareback,*
First Method

It is also possible to mount bareback by leading the horse alongside a fence and sliding onto his back. This may work well as long as there is a fence nearby and the horse will stand quietly beside it while you mount, but if you want to dismount at some point and then must rely on finding a fence to remount, you may find yourself with a long walk home, leading your horse. Therefore it will prove useful to learn one or both of the other methods of mounting bareback.

MOUNTING BY VAULTING OVER THE CROUP OF THE HORSE

Cowboy movies sometimes show a rider making a quick getaway by running behind his horse, putting both hands on the horse's croup, and vaulting into the saddle. It looks like fun and appears safe enough in the movies. Unfortunately, it is not safe, as any horse, even the quietest, may kick, and if you are directly behind him when he does, you could suffer a serious accident. Do not risk permanent injury for a few moments of fun.

Dismounting

I t is important to remember to hold onto the reins as you dismount. A horse may move off just as easily while you are getting off as while you are getting on. There are several ways of dismounting, each with advantages and disadvantages.

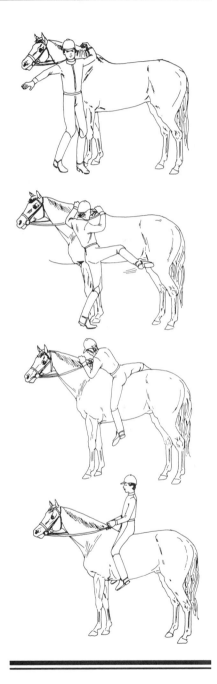

FIGURE 32B: *Mounting Bareback, Second Method*

THE USUAL WAY OF DISMOUNTING

To dismount in the usual way (see figure 33a) transfer the reins to your left hand. Place your left hand, holding the reins with your fingers or knuckles pointing toward the off (right) side of the horse, across the crest of the neck, just in front of the withers. Have your whip in your left hand, hanging down at the horse's near (left) shoulder. Stand in the stirrups, placing your right hand on the right knee roll or on the pommel to help keep your balance; swing your right leg over the croup, taking care not to touch the horse; and bring your right leg alongside the left one. Supporting your full weight on your hands (the left hand continues to hold the reins on the neck while the right moves to the seat of the saddle), remove your left foot from the stirrup. Your stomach is now against the horse's side. Now, turn your right hip toward the horse and push slightly away from him so that your clothes, and especially your belt buckle, do not scrape the saddle as you dismount. Then drop lightly to the ground. Be sure not to let go of the reins, and take care to avoid the horse's front legs as you land. Take the reins over the horse's head immediately upon dismounting so that he cannot pull back and break loose. Hold the buckle of the reins in your left hand and the reins about six to ten inches below the bit in your right hand for leading. Run both stirrup irons up (see figure 17, page 42) so that they cannot hit you or the horse. The girth should be loosened a few holes if you do not intend to remount right away.

DISMOUNTING USING ONE STIRRUP IRON

It is useful to know how to dismount using one stirrup iron should terrain or foot injury prevent dismounting in the usual manner. The method involves keeping one foot in the stirrup as you lower the other to the ground. However, using one iron can be dangerous; at the moment when one foot is in the stirrup and the other on the ground, the rider is in a vulnerable position and could lose his balance if the horse moves. In a freak accident, the rider, unable to remove his or her foot from the stirrup, could be dragged if the horse should panic or shy.

The method is as follows (see figure 33b), but should be used only if it cannot be avoided: Take the reins in the left hand, along with a handful of

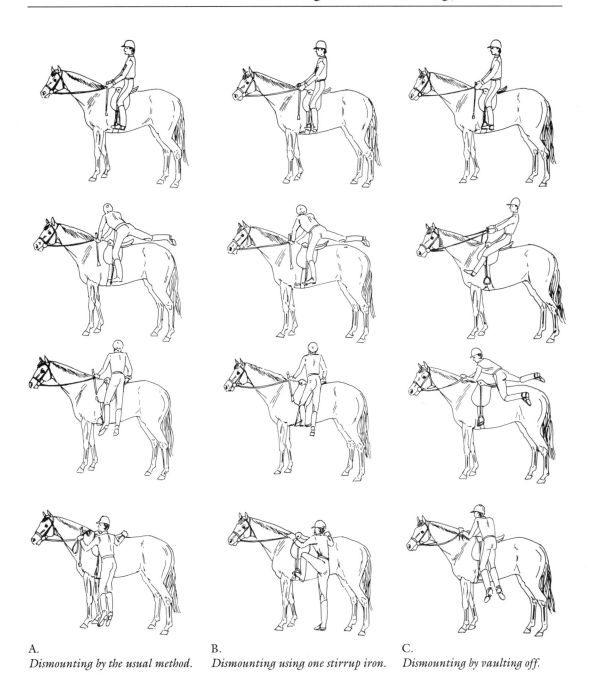

A.
Dismounting by the usual method.

B.
Dismounting using one stirrup iron.

C.
Dismounting by vaulting off.

FIGURE 33:   **Dismounting**

mane. The whip is also in the left hand, hanging down alongside the horse's shoulder. Put your right hand on the knee roll or pommel for balance. Stand in the irons, swing your right leg over the croup, being careful not to touch it, and bring your right leg alongside the left one (which is still in the left stirrup iron). At the same time, move your hand from the right knee roll or pommel to the cantle of the saddle, instead of supporting your weight by pushing down on the seat of the saddle.

Keeping your left foot in the stirrup, lower your right foot to the ground. This is the most vulnerable moment, because if the horse takes a step forward, sideways, or backward, you will have an awkward and difficult time keeping your balance. While your left hand is on the reins and neck and your right hand on the cantle to help you to control the horse and maintain your balance in the event the horse moves, remove your left foot from the stirrup promptly so that there is no possibility of your foot getting caught in it. Bring the reins over the horse's head and run the irons up in the usual way. The girth should be loosened if you do not intend to remount right away.

DISMOUNTING BY VAULTING OFF

Vaulting off is a useful emergency procedure and is the fastest way of getting off a horse.

To vault off (see figure 33c, page 73) place your left hand, holding the reins and a handful of mane, across the horse's neck about eight inches above the withers, with your fingers pointing toward the right side of the horse. Put your right hand on the pommel. Remove both feet from the stirrups. Let both legs swing forward toward the horse's shoulders as you lean backward slightly with your upper body; then in one decisive movement, swing both legs backward and your upper body forward toward the crest of the horse's neck. Your right leg will swing clear of the horse's croup, and both legs will come together as you drop to the ground. Push yourself far enough from the horse so that you do not scrape against the saddle with your belt buckle. Land lightly on the balls of your feet, facing forward, and be sure to hold onto the reins. Practice vaulting off on *both* sides of the horse.

This method of dismounting can be practiced first at a standstill, and later at the walk, trot, and canter. A horse will generally stop quickly from any gait when he feels the rider vault off his back in this manner.

DISMOUNTING BY SLIDING OFF THE HORSE'S CROUP

Dismounting by sliding off over the horse's rump is the counterpart to mounting by vaulting on over his croup and should *not* be practiced. If a horse, even the quietest, becomes startled or frightened, his first reaction is to run. If you are near his hind feet when he wants to run, there is a very good chance he will try to kick you out of the way. A direct kick from a horse can cause serious injury.

DISMOUNTING BY SWINGING YOUR RIGHT LEG OVER THE WITHERS

It is unwise to practice dismounting by bringing your right leg over the withers in front of the saddle (rather than by bringing it over the horse's croup in the usual way), unless someone else is holding the horse for you, because this places you in an unbalanced position at the moment that you must let go of the reins entirely. If the horse makes a sudden movement, you could lose your balance and the horse could leave you on the ground.

DISMOUNTING FROM THE WRONG (OFF) SIDE

To dismount from the wrong (off) side, follow the instructions for dismounting in the usual way or for using one stirrup iron, but in each case substitute left for right. You should become equally confident dismounting from either side, and the time it takes to learn to do so will be well spent.

Falls

Every rider has falls from his or her horse, and most experienced riders have at some time had a horse fall down with them. The vast majority of falls result in nothing more than a momentary interruption of the ride and perhaps some joking comments from your friends.

But some falls can be dangerous, and as a rider you must know how to fall and what to do as soon as you feel that either you are parting company with the horse, or the horse is going down with you.

WHEN THE HORSE FALLS DOWN

Of the two falls, those in which the horse goes down with the rider (falling to his knees or even on his side) tend to be the more dangerous. If you feel the horse begin to stumble back or buckle at the knees, immediately vault off on whichever side is best depending on terrain. Do not wait to see whether the horse is really going to fall; if you even *think* he may be falling, vault off without hesitation. You can always remount, but you cannot always suffer such a fall without injury.

In the course of any fall, do your best to stay out of the way of the horse's hooves. A horse will make every effort to avoid stepping on a person, but in the confusion of the moment he may inadvertently do so. The greatest danger occurs when the horse scrambles to get on his feet again. If you are near his feet, he may step on you. This is particularly true if you are near his hind legs, which have much more mobility and provide most of the power he uses to get up again. It is also more difficult for the horse to see you there. Turn your head so that your hard hat, not your face, is toward the probable direction of his hoof movement, and speak to the horse to help him know your position relative to his own.

WHEN YOU ARE THROWN FROM THE HORSE

If the horse does not fall but you lose your balance and begin to come off him, immediately vault off. If you can hold onto the reins, do so, but do not risk injury by hanging onto them at all cost. It is better to have to catch a loose horse or even to have to walk home than it is to inadvertently pull a horse down on top of you by the reins.

If you are thrown headfirst from the horse and have no time to vault off, roll yourself up as much as possible into a ball as you fall; your arms especially should not protrude, but should be wrapped loosely around your body. A fall that happens so quickly that the rider has no time to try to break it with an outstretched arm is usually the safest. Attempting to break your fall with your hands can result in a broken arm or collarbone. Try to hit the ground rolling; in any case, when you hit the ground, immediately roll away from the horse. Do not attempt to hold onto the reins if you are thrown; the speed and the downward direction in which you are thrown make it nearly impossible to do so safely.

Before you remount, examine the horse (if he has fallen) and yourself for injury. Remount if both of you are reasonably intact. If either has suffered a substantial injury of any kind, do not attempt to ride, but seek help from companions or anyone else nearby. If you think you may have suffered a concussion or a severe blow to the head, do not remount under any circumstances. "Getting right back on the horse" is *not* invariably the best policy and discretion should be exercised.

QUIZ

1. Before you mount a horse, you should always
   (A) ask an assistant to hold the horse
   (B) check the tack carefully whether or not someone else has saddled the horse for you
   (C) have another person check the tack for you

2. When leading a bridled horse, you should always
   (A) bring the reins over the horse's head, holding the reins six to ten inches below the bit with your right hand, with the buckle end of the reins in your left hand
   (B) leave the reins where they normally lie on the horse's neck, just in front of the withers
   (C) remove the bridle and put on a halter instead

3. When you first put on the saddle, the girth should be
   (A) done up as tightly as possible
   (B) done up just tightly enough so the saddle stays on while you lead the horse to the place where you will mount
   (C) done up tightly enough so that you can fit one or two fingers between the girth and the horse's side

4. The throatlatch of the bridle should be buckled
   (A) as tightly as you can conveniently get it
   (B) very loosely
   (C) loosely at first, and tightened later

5. When mounting, your whip should be held in
   (A) the right hand
   (B) the left hand
   (C) neither hand; an assistant should hand it to you when you are in the saddle

6. When you are mounted and holding the reins correctly, the extra rein that falls between your hands is called
   (A) the crupper
   (B) the false rein
   (C) the bight

7. When mounting from the ground, at the moment just prior to springing upward into the saddle, you should face the direction of the horse's
   (A) hip
   (B) side
   (C) shoulder

8. The reins of a snaffle bridle pass between your
   (A) first and second fingers
   (B) two middle fingers
   (C) ring and little fingers

9. The bight of the reins should fall on the
   (A) off side   (B) near side

10. When using a pelham bit, there will be
    (A) a single rein on each side of the horse's neck
    (B) double reins on each side of the horse's neck
    (C) neither of the above

11. When holding the reins, how much bend should the rider's wrists have?
    (A) forty-five-degree angle
    (B) ten-degree angle
    (C) none

12. When adjusting the stirrups from the ground, a rough guide for judging the correct length is
    (A) make the stirrup leathers the length equal to one-third of your height
    (B) the bottom of the stirrup irons should come exactly to the bottom line of the horse's belly
    (C) the length of the stirrup leather and the stirrup should equal the length of your outstretched arm to the knuckles of your fingers

(continued next page)

QUIZ

(continued)

13. When adjusting the stirrups from a mounted position in the saddle, a rough guide for judging the correct length is
    (A) when your knees are in line with your ankle when viewed from above, they are properly adjusted
    (B) the bottom of the stirrup iron should hit your ankle bone when your leg hangs straight down in a relaxed position
    (C) your toe should just reach the top of the stirrup iron when you let your heel drop as low as it will go

14. *True or false:* Use of a mounting block is the best way to mount in most cases.

15. *True or false:* It is a good idea to learn to mount and dismount on the "wrong" (off) side of the horse.

16. Mounting with the assistance of another person who lifts you into the air high enough for you to swing your right leg over the horse's croup is called
    (A) using the aids
    (B) getting a leg up
    (C) the bareback method

17. When should you mount and dismount by vaulting over the croup of a horse?
    (A) only on a very quiet horse
    (B) if you are very athletic
    (C) never

18. When should you dismount by keeping your left foot in the stirrup until your right foot has touched the ground?
    (A) always
    (B) never
    (C) only if terrain or injury to a foot prevents dismounting in the usual way

19. When you dismount in the usual way, be careful that
    (A) your whip is in your right hand
    (B) your belt buckle does not scrape the saddle
    (C) your reins are adjusted as tightly as possible

20. If your horse begins to fall, you should
    (A) roll with the horse
    (B) hold onto the reins at all cost
    (C) vault off

21. *True or false:* After a fall, it is always the best policy to "get right back on the horse."

Answers: 1B, 2A, 3B, 4B, 5B, 6C, 7A, 8C, 9A, 10B, 11C, 12C, 13B, 14. false, 15. true, 16B, 17C, 18C, 19B, 20C, 21. false.

7

The Rider's Position

The Importance of Position

Although *position*, how the rider sits on the horse, is a means to an end and not an end in itself, a beginning rider will spend a good deal of time learning to sit correctly, first at the halt, walk, and trot, and later at the canter, gallop, and while jumping. The rider's position and the use of the aids at all gaits should first be practiced in a quiet, enclosed area, such as a fenced ring or indoor arena.

In order to give the aids (signals) to the horse correctly and with precision, the rider's hands, legs, and weight must be in the correct position.

There is not, in fact, only one "correct position," but many. Which of these many positions the rider takes depends upon the gait (walk, trot, canter, gallop), the speed at which the horse is traveling, whether his head and neck are elevated or extended, and whether he is going uphill, downhill, or on the flat. In each case, the horse's center of gravity will be different, and the rider must change his or her own center of gravity accordingly to keep in balance with the horse. Each of these specific positions will be explained in detail in chapters 9 and 10.

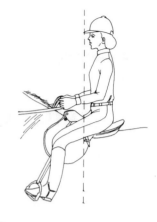

A.
Incorrect: Heels too far behind rider cause rider to tip forward.

B.
Correct: Ear, shoulder, hip, heel in alignment—rider is in a position ready to move with the horse.

C.
Incorrect: Heels pushed too far in front of rider causes rider's weight to be thrown backward. (Riders sometimes push their heels too far forward in an effort to lower them.)

FIGURE 34:   ***Position of the Rider***

The rider's position in the saddle is secured not by gripping the horse with his or her legs, but by proper distribution of body weight. A rider's position must be easily adaptable to any change in the horse's center of gravity. This position, once learned, will be graceful and in fluid harmony with the movements of the horse.

The Overall Position

The overall outline of your body when on a horse should be that of a person standing on the ground with both knees slightly bent and feet about two and one-half feet apart. Your ear, shoulder, hip and heel should be in alignment. If your feet are too far behind you (see figure 34a), your body will be prone to tip forward; if they are too far in front (see figure 34c), you will be prone to lose your balance backward. Therefore, the correct position of the legs is of prime importance (see figure 34b).

The way in which you prevent your upper body from being thrown forward is by pushing down on your heels and/or pushing them forward. You prevent being thrown backward by closing your hip angle and leaning forward.

Your legs should not grip the horse's sides by force. Rather, they should lie against the horse so that your weight pushes you securely and deeply into the saddle and places your thighs closely against the horse's sides in a position requiring no effort to maintain.

To position your legs correctly, reach down with your hand and grasp the *back* part of your thigh, pull it outward,

Incorrect: Rider gripping saddle with the back part of the thigh, which pulls the knee away from the saddle.

Correct: Draw the back part of thigh away from the saddle, then release it. This places the inner front part *of the thigh correctly against the saddle.*

FIGURE 35:   *Position of the Rider's Leg*

away from the saddle, then release it (see figure 35). Do this with each thigh. You will find that your weight now rests primarily on the *inside* part of your thighs or even on the *inside front* part. Never allow the *back* parts of your thighs to grip the saddle; notice that if they do, your knees will automatically fall outward, away from the saddle (see figure 36). If this happens while you are riding, you may at first need to adjust your position with your hands as described; later you will be able to turn your thighs inward from the top without using your hand.

Do not ride too long at first; ten or fifteen minutes on each of the first few days is plenty. Increase the duration little by little; your inner thigh muscles need to gradually learn to become supple enough to conform to the shape of the horse, and you may undergo considerable discomfort if you try to rush the process. By riding too long at first, you may simply make your legs so sore that you cannot sit properly at all; or, because of the strain, you may *think* you are sitting correctly when actually you are not. No good purpose is served by rid-

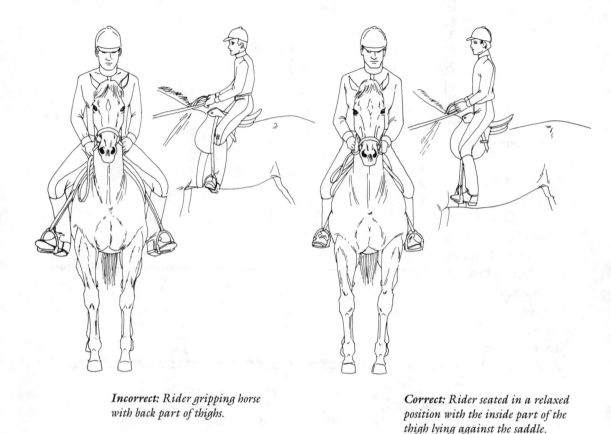

Incorrect: Rider gripping horse with back part of thighs.

Correct: Rider seated in a relaxed position with the inside part of the thigh lying against the saddle.

FIGURE 36:   ***Position of the Rider's Leg***

ing for a longer period of time than you can practice correctly. Bad habits, once learned, are difficult to overcome; you will establish a sound position most quickly by riding only as long as you can practice correctly.

Your *knees* should not grip the saddle. They should lie lightly against it, as is natural when the thighs are properly positioned.

Your *seat* is correctly placed when your seat bones feel the saddle, with the fleshy part of your buttocks placed *behind* you rather than under you. Never tuck your seat under you and sit on its fleshy part, as this will cause you to perch on top of the horse in an insecure position rather than to sink deeply down into the saddle.

Your *calves* should lie gently against the horse's sides. They should not grip; they stay in place simply by their weight. They remain in this position until needed to give specific signals. Like your knees, your calves will fall naturally into place if your upper thighs are positioned correctly.

Your *heels* must rest as low as you can get them, at least an inch or two lower than the toes, without pushing your feet forward in the effort to bring your heels down. The lower your heels are, the lower your calves will be. Your calves should rest as low as possible on the horse's sides, allowing more surface in contact with the horse with which to give the aids (signals) to him. The stirrup leathers should hang straight down when your heels are pushed down.

The lower your heels, the more flexible your ankle joint and better your ankle can function as a shock absorber. Every time the horse stops or slows down even slightly, your ankle joint must absorb the shock by bending more sharply, to prevent your upper body from pitching forward. By always keeping your heels well down, you will establish the position that will best prevent you from being thrown off balance when the horse *checks* (slows) his speed.

In addition, by keeping your heels down, you minimize the possibility of accidentally slipping a foot through a stirrup iron, which could cause you to be dragged in the event of a fall.

Your *feet* should either point straight ahead or be turned very slightly outward. They must not be held out at an exaggerated angle by force.

Your *back* should be tall and straight, but not stiff. It may be *very* slightly arched, but must never be hunched. If you concentrate on bringing your chest as high as comfortably possible, your back will position itself correctly.

Your *upper arms* should rest lightly against your sides, but slant slightly forward so that the elbow joint is in front of your body, or lightly against the front part of your rib cage.

Your *lower arms* should form a straight line from elbow to bit when seen from above or from the side (see figure 29, page 65). Your wrists should not be bent.

Your *hands* should continue the line of the lower arms, with the fingers loosely curled. They hold the reins as shown in figure 28, page 64.

Your *head* should be carried high but with the chin brought gently inward rather than poked out in front. Your *eyes* should look ahead rather than down at the horse's head and neck. They should scan the line that you intend to ride and be alert for potential trouble such as closeness to other horses, traffic, or objects that might frighten the horse.

THE RIDER'S POSITION WHILE RIDING BAREBACK

There are two ways to ride bareback. The first requires that you adopt the same position you would in a saddle; this is a frequent test for horsemanship at horse shows. The second method, useful for improving balance, is to let your entire leg fall fully relaxed, with your toes lower than your heels. Do not ride a horse bareback if he has a tendency to bolt, as it may be difficult to stop him.

Suppling Exercises

All suppling exercises serve to improve your balance and coordination while mounted. Practicing them for a few minutes is a useful way to feel more comfortable and at home on a horse. However, be sure to have someone hold the horse while you do them, as your movements in the saddle may inadvertently cause the horse to move when you least expect it.

DROPPING AND REGAINING THE STIRRUP IRONS

Lift your feet out of the stirrups, let your legs hang down as low as possible, toes pointing downward, then regain your stirrups by raising your feet, turning your toes inward toward the horse, and inserting your feet in the irons. Practice at the halt and at the walk, ten times each.

TOUCHING YOUR TOES

Reach down with your left hand and touch your left toe. Reach down with your right hand and touch your right toe. Repeat ten times.

Next, reach across the horse and touch your left toe with your right hand; then touch your right toe with your left hand. Repeat ten times at the halt and at the walk.

LEANING FORWARD AND BACKWARD

Lean forward until your head touches the horse's mane. Then lean back until your head touches his croup. Repeat five times at the halt.

PIVOTING FROM THE WAIST

Hold both arms straight out, parallel to the ground. Without moving your legs, twist at the waist as far as you can to the right to face the tail of the horse; then twist around as far as you can to the left toward the tail of the horse. Repeat twenty times at the halt and at the walk.

QUIZ

1. The rider's position is important because
   (A) position is the most important end result of riding
   (B) the rider's hands, legs, and weight must be in the best position to give the aids effectively
   (C) there is only one correct position

2. *True or false:* The rider's leg grip is ninety percent of the correct position on a horse.

3. The correct position for the rider's upper leg is
   (A) with the back part of the thigh gripping the saddle
   (B) with the front or inside front part of the thigh lying against the saddle
   (C) neither of the above

4. The correct position for the rider's seat is with
   (A) the buttocks tucked beneath the rider
   (B) the weight of the rider pushing the seat bones deeply into the saddle
   (C) the seat bones tucked as far under the rider as possible

5. *True or false:* To learn quickly, a beginning rider should practice his or her position for an hour daily without fail.

6. The rider's heels should be
   (A) level with the toes
   (B) higher than the toes
   (C) lower than the toes

7. The primary joint that prevents the rider's upper body from pitching forward if the horse slows or stops is the
   (A) ankle
   (B) knee
   (C) calf

8. *True or false:* The rider's feet should turn outward at a minimum of a forty-five-degree angle.

9. Suppling exercises should be practiced
   (A) for at least an hour daily
   (B) with someone holding the horse's head in case he moves
   (C) only by people who are exceptionally timid about horses

Answers: 1B, 2. false, 3B, 4B, 5. false 6C, 7A, 8. false, 9B.

8

The Aids: How to Communicate with Your Horse

THE WORD *aids*, as it applies to riding, has two separate meanings. First, it means the *signals* that a rider gives a horse to ask him to do something. This is the usual meaning of the term—for example, "the aids for the canter" or "the aids for the trot."

The second definition of *aids* is the *physical means used by a rider to enforce these signals*. Within this category are two groups: the *natural aids* are legs, hands, weight, and voice, and the *artificial aids* are whips, spurs, martingales, and so forth. The bridle and saddle are not considered artificial aids, but everything else used to influence a horse's way of going is.

The aids must be used as lightly as possible to accomplish the desired effect. *When the horse responds correctly, the aid must cease instantly. If the aid is ignored or disobeyed, the rider must enforce it* with either the natural aids, the artificial aids, or both.

The Natural Aids

THE RIDER'S LEGS

The horse's power comes almost entirely from his hind legs, which are governed by the strong muscles of the haunches. The hind legs move not only backward and forward, as do the front legs, but can also easily move sideways. In a sense, the horse's hind legs are the engine upon which he depends for his power. For example, a horse may use his front legs to strike at another horse, but if he wants to deliver a well-placed blow that will disable an adversary, he will invariably spin around and use his hind legs.

The rider's legs "speak" directly to the horse's hind legs. The rider's left leg influences the horse's left hind leg; his right leg influences the right.

The rider's legs, used simultaneously at the girth, direct the horse to create energetic forward movement called *impulsion*.

The rider's legs can also move the horse sideways or prevent sideways movement. For example, the left leg, used four inches behind the girth, will move the horse's hindquarters away from the pressure; that is, to the right. In this way, the hindquarters can be guided and controlled.

The rider's legs can act passively, by simply resting against the horse's sides without making any demands, or actively, by a tightening of the calf muscles, or by squeezing inward. If necessary, the rider can reinforce the leg aids by using one or more of the artificial aids, such as whip or spurs.

To give the leg aids, you should first merely *tighten your calf muscles.* This, to a well-schooled horse, provides a clear signal to move forward in any of several ways, depending upon what aids are given simultaneously by the hands. It is wrong to assume that because a horse makes no response to the tightening of your calves he has failed to feel the signal. A simple test will prove this: place your own hand, flat, between your calf and the horse's side. Tighten your calf muscle without squeezing your leg against the horse's side. Notice how clearly this can be felt. The horse can feel it too, but only a well-schooled horse will respond to it.

If the horse fails to respond to tightening of the calves, your immediate action should be to repeat the signal, adding a distinct inward squeeze with your legs against the horse's sides. At the same time, apply a sharp, stinging tap with the whip as close behind your calf as possible. To the horse, it feels as if the sting actually originated from your leg.

The important point here is that a good rider never uses a severe aid initially. First, the mildest aid possible is used, although it must always be perfectly clear. Only if the aid is disregarded or disobeyed does the rider follow with an aid of more severity. In this way, the horse soon realizes that it is to his own advantage to respond promptly to the mild aid (causing the signal to cease immediately), while disobedience only brings the swift application of a more severe aid.

THE RIDER'S HANDS

The rider's hands regulate the impulsion (energetic forward movement) created by the horse's hind legs. They can move the *forehand* (the front half of the horse) to either side or prevent that movement; they can slow or stop the forward movement of the horse or allow it to flow freely. *Free forward movement is essential to all riding.*

The horse's forelegs, unlike his hind legs, move for the most part only forward and backward, with very little sideways movement possible. In a sense, the forelegs merely line themselves up with the hind legs, which actually do most of the steering. Therefore a rider should eventually learn to control the horse more and more with the legs and less and less with the hands.

The rider's hands act on the reins, which act on the bit in the horse's mouth. Placement of the horse's head and neck greatly affect his center of gravity. The rider can control placement of the head and neck to a large extent via the reins.

Your hands can be either active or passive. When active, your hands exert pressure on the reins, either by a squeezing of the fingers (like the motion of squeezing water from a sponge), or by resisting the horse if he pushes his nose slightly forward to ask for more rein. If necessary, your hands can also move in a backward direction: that is, from slightly in front of the withers to somewhat behind them. To do this, bring your elbows back. As with all the aids, however, the mildest aid should always be given first, followed by more severe aids only if the signal is disregarded or disobeyed.

When active, your hands may also act in any of several ways to turn, slow, or stop the horse. Each of these possibilities will be explained separately in chapter 9, which discusses each gait.

When passive, your hands follow the movement of the horse's head so that you maintain the lightest possible contact with his mouth. How your hands move, and when, will also be explained separately in the sections on each gait in chapter 9.

"GOOD HANDS"

One of the greatest compliments a rider can receive is to be told that he or she has "good hands." What exactly does "good hands" mean? What do they do, or not do? How can you develop them?

Good hands do the following: First, they give the correct aids clearly at the right moment. Second, they use a signal as light as possible, but as strong as necessary to get the correct response. Third, and most important, they *cease giving the aids the instant the horse responds*. Good hands do *not* "give and take" on the reins indiscriminately—that is, *they do not release pressure before the horse has done what is required*.

The principles of good hands hold true for any rider, from the rank beginner to the Grand Prix dressage rider or Olympic world champion. A beginning rider needs only a general awareness of the refinement possible in the rein aids given by an expert rider to a well-schooled horse. The keys to developing good hands are, first, *to become increasingly sensitive to the moment the horse begins to respond*, and second, *to then instantly cease giving the aids*.

THE RIDER'S WEIGHT

There are two objectives to the rider's adopting a given position on the horse: to make the rider more efficient, and to make the horse more efficient. The rider must find the point at which his or her own center of gravity is balanced directly above that of the horse. Only when these two centers of gravity are in accord can the rider give the aids with precision, and can the horse move with maximum efficiency.

If the rider's center of gravity is different from the horse's, he or she will feel out of balance; either "behind the movement" or "in front of the movement" of the horse. Because the horse's center of gravity changes constantly and fluidly, depending upon what he is doing (see figure 37), the rider should not remain in one static position but rather in many different positions that also change continually to adapt to the horse's center of gravity.

Try the following experiment (see figure 38). Sit in a straight-backed chair with both feet planted on the floor in front of you, about twenty inches apart. Keeping your feet on the floor, try to rise up as though you were posting at the trot (see *The Posting Trot*, page 107) while riding and, at the same time, attempt to squeeze inward with your lower leg from knee to ankle as though you were giving the aids to a horse to move forward. You will find that because your center of gravity is too far back, both actions will be extremely difficult, if not impossible, to carry out. Now bring your legs back along either side of the chair until your ear, shoulder, hip, and heel are in alignment. Repeat the posting action and the leg action. You will find that if you modify your position by leaning slightly forward you will be in the correct position to post and to give the aids without difficulty.

Now consider the effect of the rider's center of gravity on the horse. If the rider's center of gravity is different from the horse's, the horse must expend substantial energy simply fighting this imbalance. Another test will demonstrate this point: give another person a "piggyback ride" on your own back. If you attempt to do this while standing straight up, you will be unable to maintain your balance without taking some quick steps back-

1

During the first beat of the gallop, the horse brings his hind legs underneath his body, his head and neck come up slightly and the center of gravity momentarily shifts backward.

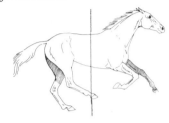

2

During the late second beat and all of the third beat of the gallop, the horse's head and neck are fully extended, and the center of gravity is forward.

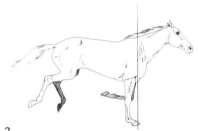

3

During the fourth beat of the gallop, the horse's center of gravity is far forward.

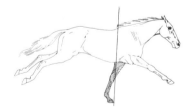

How It Changes Depending on the Beat of the Gait

FIGURE 37: *The Horse's Center of Gravity*

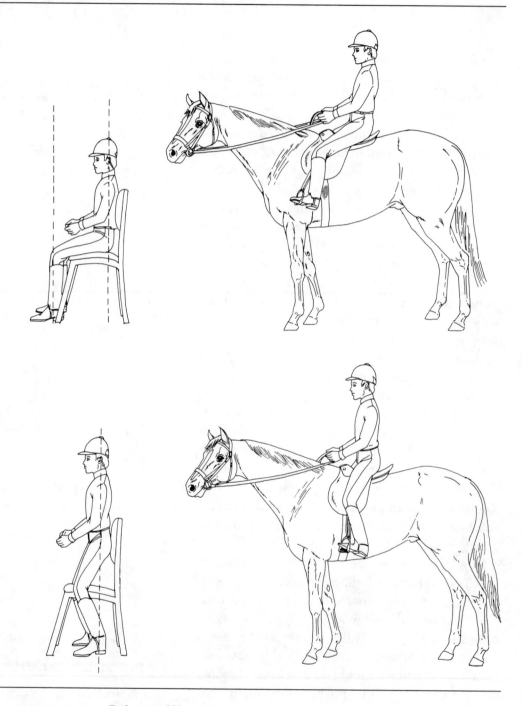

FIGURE 38:   *Balance while posting*

ward to keep from falling. If you lean forward, though, you will find a point at which you and your "rider" are in balance: You will find that you can most easily move in any direction when both your centers of gravity are in accord. Now have your "rider" lean backward or sideways while you continue to maintain your position. As soon as the accord between your centers of gravity is disrupted, you will begin to lose your balance and be forced to expend energy to regain it. In the case of a rider and a horse, the principle is the same (see figure 39).

The point is that the rider must take a position on a horse from which he or she can readily change his or her center of gravity to conform to that of the horse. There is no such thing as one "correct position" on a horse, because the horse is capable of many different movements. Each movement has a different center of gravity for the horse; each requires a different center of gravity and, hence, a different position in the rider.

However, there is one position from which the rider can most easily adapt his or her own center of gravity to that of the horse: the position placing the rider's ear, a shoulder, hip, and heel in alignment (see figure 40).

THE RIDER'S VOICE

The voice can be used to soothe, encourage, or scare a horse into obedience. It should be used when needed, but must not replace the aids given by legs, hands, and weight. A good general rule is to use your voice only when the same effect cannot be accomplished by either the natural or the artificial aids.

The Artificial Aids

The two artificial aids with which a beginning rider should be concerned are the whip and the standing martingale.

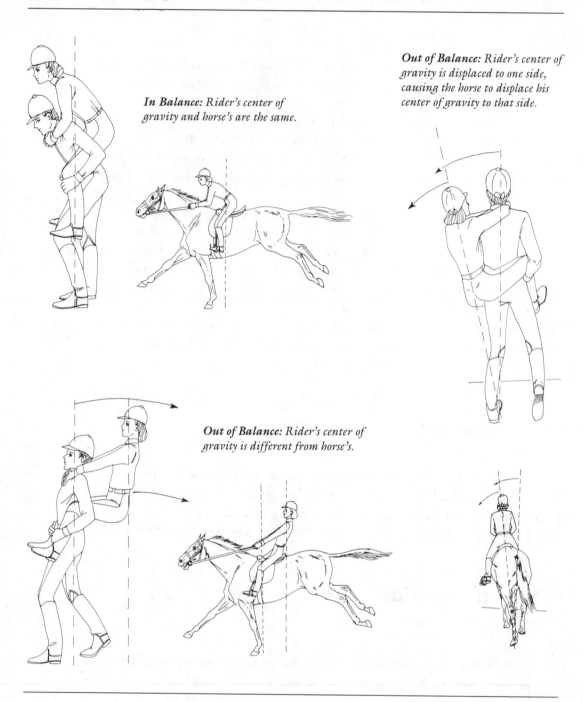

In Balance: *Rider's center of gravity and horse's are the same.*

Out of Balance: *Rider's center of gravity is displaced to one side, causing the horse to displace his center of gravity to that side.*

Out of Balance: *Rider's center of gravity is different from horse's.*

FIGURE 39:   ***Rider's center of gravity***

Standing
Head elevated.
Hocks beneath body.
Horse and rider
have same center
of gravity.

Trotting
1. Collected trot.
   Hocks beneath the
   horse's body.
   Rider's center of
   gravity is aligned
   with the horse's
   when the rider sits
   straight.

2. Extended trot.
   Head extended.
   Rider's center of
   gravity moves for-
   ward to remain
   in equilibrium.

Walking
1. Rider feels
   himself thrust
   backward as horse
   begins to move
   forward into the
   walk.

2. Head extended.
   Center of gravity
   of horse is in
   front of rider's.
   Rider must adopt
   a forward seat to
   remain in
   equilibrium.

3. At an ordinary
   walk, the center
   of gravity of horse
   and rider are at
   equilibrium.

Cantering
Collected canter.
Head elevated.
Centers of gravity of
horse and rider are
in line.

Full Gallop
Head and neck
greatly extended.
Rider leans forward
to remain in equilibrium
with the horse's center
of gravity.

Courbette
The horse's center of
gravity is moved
back. Rider's center
of gravity remains
in equilibrium
with the horse's.

Rearing
Rider throws his
own weight forward
to influence horse
to lower his
forehand.

**Horse resisting
rein aids**
Head elevated.
Center of gravity of
horse and rider are
out of alignment.

Uphill
Center of gravity of
horse and rider
shifts forward.

Downhill
Center of gravity of
horse and rider
shifts backward.

FIGURE 40: *How changes in terrain and gate alter the horse's center of gravity, requiring the rider to adapt his own center of gravity accordingly.*

A

The whip carried in the left hand.

B

The left hand holds both reins and whip while the right hand reaches for top of whip and pulls it through the left hand, then carries it across to the right side of the horse.

C

The right hand places the whip across the right knee, and takes up the right rein in the usual way.

FIGURE 41: ***Changing the Whip from One Hand to the Other***

THE WHIP

The whip is used to reinforce a leg aid that has been ignored or disobeyed. It must be carried every time you ride, because a horse must never be allowed to refuse to go forward. It is generally held in the inside hand when riding in a ring, unless a specific purpose calls for its use on the outside. (*Inside* refers to the inside of a turn or circle. When riding in a clockwise direction, the inside hand is the right hand, and the outside hand is the left.)

The usual way to hold the whip is with the long part pointing downward, resting it across your knee when it's not in active use (see figure 41a). About two to four inches of whip should protrude above your hand, and six or more inches should protrude below the point at which the whip rests on your knee.

To change the whip from one hand to the other, take both reins in the hand that already holds the whip (see figures 41b and 41c). With your free hand reach across and take the whip by the top part (above the hand), lift it carefully upward, drawing it through the hand holding the reins, and place it on your other knee, taking up the reins in the normal way. Do not wave it around during the process, as this may frighten the horse. Keep enough tension on the reins so that the horse does not hurry forward as you change the whip from one hand to the other.

While riding on trails (*hacking*), or across country, you should change the whip from one hand to the other from time to time so that the horse becomes accustomed to its presence on either side, and you become equally adept at holding it in either hand.

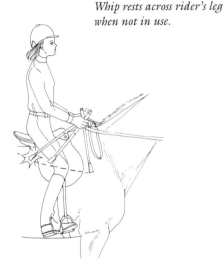

Whip rests across rider's leg when not in use.

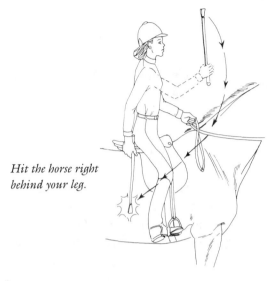

Hit the horse right behind your leg.

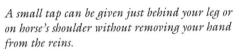

A small tap can be given just behind your leg or on horse's shoulder without removing your hand from the reins.

If the whip is held in the reversed position, it can be used forcefully with maximum effectiveness. However, beginning riders are cautioned that this use may cause a sudden reaction in the horse.

FIGURE 42:   ***Three Inches of Whip Extends Above Hand***

If your horse refuses to go forward when asked, use your whip as you repeat the aids (squeeze with your calves). Tap the horse—about as hard as you can hit your bare arm without producing very much pain—directly behind your leg, as close to your calf as possible, so that it feels to the horse as though the sting came from your leg. The whip must be used the instant the horse disobeys the leg aids; do not delay in hopes that the horse will somehow obey you if you merely repeat the leg aids without using the whip. Failure to use the whip at the moment of disobedience is a serious riding fault because doing so teaches the horse that he can disobey the leg aids with impunity. The less time elapsing between the disobedience and the use of the whip, the better.

The sequence is as follows: Use your leg aids (tighten your calf muscles and squeeze) to tell the horse to go forward. If the horse ignores or disobeys the aids by failing to respond or by moving backward, immediately repeat the leg aids, exactly as before, and at the same time apply a sharp tap with the whip directly behind your calf (see figure 42).

If the horse disobeys by moving sideways, apply the whip on that side. For example, if you are passing an open gate on your right and the horse attempts to duck through it, hit the horse on the right side to drive him away from the gate. As soon as you have used the whip it should be replaced across your knee.

If a very strong swat is necessary to correct a particularly stubborn horse, the whip should be turned in the hand so that the long part is pointing upward. When used in this way, it can give a severe, stinging punishment. But a beginning rider must not attempt to use the whip in this way until his or her seat is firmly established, since most horses react suddenly to this measure and may attempt to run off. In fact, a beginning rider should be sure that when he or she uses the whip it is not inadvertently turned upside down.

In general merely carrying a whip, without using it, sufficiently reminds most horses that the leg aids must be obeyed. The whip must never be used around a horse's head, as it can injure his eyes and will make him headshy.

THE STANDING MARTINGALE

The standing martingale should be used with any horse who habitually raises his head above the bit in order to avoid responding correctly to the rein aids. A martingale does not actually change the horse's mental attitude—he will still attempt to avoid obeying the reins—but it does prevent him from raising his head above the point where the reins can influence him (see *The Standing Martingale*, page 45, and figure 20).

SPURS

The beginning rider need not be concerned with spurs, which are used to add impetus to the leg aids. Until the rider's leg position is firmly established, there is a good chance he or she will accidentally jab the horse with spurs.

QUIZ

1. The word *aids*, as it applies to riding, has two meanings. They are
   - (A) signals a rider gives a horse
   - (B) assistance a rider gives another rider
   - (C) physical means used by a rider to enforce signals previously given to a horse
   - (D) signals a rider gives another rider to indicate that he or she intends to turn, stop, and so forth

2. Legs, hands, weight, and voice are called
   - (A) artificial aids
   - (B) necessary aids
   - (C) natural aids

3. Whips and martingales are called
   - (A) equine aids
   - (B) natural aids
   - (C) artificial aids

4. The horse's power comes primarily from his
   - (A) forelegs
   - (B) hind legs
   - (C) neck and shoulder muscles

5. Energetic forward movement is called
   - (A) action
   - (B) impulsion
   - (C) movement

6. *True or false:* The rider should give the aids very strongly from the start so there is no chance that the horse will disobey.

7. *True or false:* The rider should use the aids as lightly as possible, only increasing their severity if they are ignored or disobeyed.

8. "Good hands" do which of the following?
   - (A) give clear, light signals initially
   - (B) use as much force as necessary to achieve the correct response
   - (C) "give and take" continually on the reins
   - (D) cease giving the aids the instant the horse responds correctly

9. *True or false:* The horse has one static center of gravity, the same at all gaits, and the rider must learn the correct position in the saddle to conform to it.

10. When using the whip, the rider should
    - (A) tap as close behind his or her calf as possible
    - (B) hit the horse hard once or twice on the shoulder
    - (C) tap gently several times on the horse's croup

11. For a beginning rider, the major drawback to using the whip while holding it in a reverse position in his or her hand is that
    - (A) the whip is unbalanced in this position
    - (B) the horse cannot be encouraged to move forward easily
    - (C) the horse may react suddenly to it and run off

12. For which of the following reasons should the rider's voice be used?
    - (A) to replace whenever possible the aids normally given by the reins or legs
    - (B) to soothe, encourage, or scare the horse into obedience
    - (C) to prevent the horse from relying entirely on the natural aids
    - (D) when the other natural aids alone are less effective than when used with the voice

Answers: 1A,C; 2C; 3C; 4B; 5B; 6. false; 7. true; 8A,B,D; 9. false; 10A; 11C; 12B,D.

9

The Aids for the Walk, Trot, Canter, Gallop, Halt, Turn, and Reinback

The Walk

The *walk* is a four-beat gait. Four beats make up one complete *stride*, or pace, of the walk.

The sequence (order) of footfalls is as follows: left hind, left fore, right hind, right fore (see figure 43). The beats can, for convenience, be labeled numbers one, two, three, and four. The sequence of four beats can actually begin with any foot the horse chooses, but the order in which the feet move will always remain the same. For instance, the horse may begin with the right hind food (beat three), which would then be followed by beat four (the right fore), beat one (left hind), and beat two (left fore). Or he may begin with the left fore (beat two), followed by beat three (right hind), beat four (right fore), and beat one (left hind). Another possibility would be the right fore (beat four), followed by beat one (left hind), beat two (left fore), and beat three (right hind).

As you ride at the walk, pay careful attention to the sequence of footfalls, first by looking down and checking visually and, later, simply by feel. You will soon be able to tell with complete certainty which foot of the horse is touching

There are four beats to the walk: left hind, left fore, right hind, right fore.

FIGURE 43:   *The Sequence of Footfalls at the Walk*

the ground. If you do this from the beginning of your riding career, it will be of great help to you later on, because it is important to give the aids for a change of gait (for instance, a change from a walk to a canter) at a precise moment.

The horse's head moves up and down as he walks (see figure 44). This nodding movement causes his head to be slightly closer to you when it is raised, and farther away when it is lowered. In order to follow this movement and maintain a uniformly light feel on the reins, your hands must move slightly forward and backward. This is done by allowing your elbow joints to open and close slightly.

On beats two and four, the horse requires more rein; your hands should move forward an inch or two each time the horse touches a forefoot down, and move back on the alternate beats (one and three) as the hind legs touch the ground.

THE AIDS FOR THE WALK FROM A HALT

While the horse is standing in a halt, there must be no pressure on the reins; they must be slightly slack. To go from a halt to a walk, first ease your hands forward an additional inch or two. This prevents the nodding movement of the horse's head from causing him to bump his mouth on the bit when he begins to walk forward.

A split second after you ease your hands forward, tighten the calf muscles of both legs simultaneously. If the horse moves forward in a walk, relax your calves and follow the movement of the horse's head with your hands, maintaining the lightest possible contact via the reins to the bit.

If the inward squeeze produces no response, tighten your calves and squeeze again, but also apply a sharp tap with your whip as close behind your calf as possible. The tap should be about as hard as you can hit your bare arm without producing very much pain. It should be applied as close as possible to your calf so that the horse associates the tap with the signal given by your leg. This is how you teach him to pay attention

The rider's hands move forward and back by opening and closing the angle of the elbows slightly to the follow the nodding movement of the horse's head.

FIGURE 44:   *The Walk*

to your leg. He must eventually learn to move forward in response to a mild signal from your calf alone (see *The Whip*, page 47).

Always take both reins in one hand and use the whip with the other so that you do not accidentally pull the reins as you tap the horse. When the horse walks forward, take up the reins again in the usual way.

Kicking the horse's sides rather than squeezing with your calves is *not* recommended. When you kick, your heels come up, making your position less secure. In addition, kicking does little to teach the horse to pay attention to a mild signal given properly with your legs. Kicking must not replace the proper use of your legs; rather, it is an emergency procedure for occasions when you lack the time to use your whip.

By first using the mildest aid possible (tightening the calves), followed, only if needed, by a stronger signal (inward squeeze), and, finally, a punishment (the whip), the horse soon learns the advantage of obeying the mildest aid when it first appears. To delay responding will only bring him a stronger aid, and, finally, a punishment, while to obey promptly will cause the aid to cease at once.

The Trot

The *trot* is a two-beat gait. Two beats make up one complete stride, or pace, of the trot.

The sequence of footfalls is as follows: the left hind and right fore touch the ground together, followed by the right hind and left fore together (see figure 45).

Because the hind leg on one side and the foreleg on the opposite side move at the same time, these legs are termed a *diagonal pair*. The left hind and right fore are called the *right diagonal pair*; the right hind and left fore are called the *left diagonal pair*. Note that the foreleg, not the hind leg, gives the name to the diagonal.

The trot is a springy gait and therefore difficult to sit to without bouncing, particularly if it is fast. It is customary, therefore, to rise out of the saddle during every other beat. This is called *posting* or *trot rising*.

There are two beats to the trot. The legs move in diagonal pairs. The right fore and left hind are called the right diagonal pair; *the left fore and right hind are called the* left diagonal pair.

FIGURE 45:   *The Sequence of Footfalls at the Trot*

The Posting Trot

To post, you move your seat not up and down but forward and backward, just enough to lift your buttocks off the seat of the saddle with every other beat. Do not *stand* in the stirrups to rise at the trot, or you will be too high in the air to sit in time for the second beat, and will thus fall behind the rhythm of the trot. Merely roll forward slightly on the inner part of your thighs, then sink back again on the second beat of the foot.

At the trot, the horse's center of gravity shifts slightly forward, and so must your own center of gravity. Keep your back straight or *very* slightly arched, and close the angle of your hip until you have moved your waist forward a few inches (see figure 46).

Rider inclines his body slightly forward; it moves forward and back from the thigh on every other beat (posting). Hands remain still, relative to the horse's withers. The angle of elbow opens and closes slightly.

FIGURE 46: *At the Posting Trot*

THE AIDS FOR THE TROT

The aids for the trot are the same as the aids used to go from a halt into a walk.

First, move your hands forward an inch or two so that when the horse extends his head and neck slightly to move into the trot, he will not bump against the bit. Then tighten the calves of both your legs (or use an inward squeeze, if necessary). The horse's head remains still in this gait, so once he begins to trot, keep your hands still as well. Because the horse's head comes up slightly when he trots, you may find that reins that were the right length at the walk are now too long. It is better to shorten them *after* he begins to trot than before. Many horses learn quickly that every time you shorten the reins, they will be asked to trot, and they will therefore try to trot off whenever you do so.

Sit in the saddle for the first two or three beats of the trot, then begin posting. This gives you time to look at the horse's shoulder and try to post on the correct diagonal.

DECIDING WHICH DIAGONAL TO POST ON

While riding in a ring, it is customary in the United States and Great Britain to post on the outside diagonal, that is, while riding clockwise, on the left diagonal; while riding counterclockwise, on the right diagonal. When hacking, you should change diagonals from time to time; the muscles of a horse ridden exclusively on one diagonal become stronger on that side. If this happens, the horse will develop asymmetrically and the rider will find it difficult to rise on the weaker diagonal.

TO POST ON THE LEFT DIAGONAL

Look down at the horse's left shoulder as he begins to trot. Be careful not to bend forward as you do so; just glance down with your eyes. As his left shoulder moves forward, you move forward, just lifting your seat off the seat of the saddle. As the left shoulder comes back, you sit. (Although you look at the horse's shoulder to determine the diagonal, keep in mind that not only the shoulder but also the opposite hind leg are moving at the same time.) As soon as you are sure that you are on the left diagonal, lift your eyes and look ahead. Avoid looking down longer than necessary, because it tends to pull your body out of line and make you sit crookedly.

TO POST ON THE RIGHT DIAGONAL

As the horse's right shoulder moves forward, you move forward. As it comes back, you sit.

TO CHANGE DIAGONALS WHILE TROTTING

To change from the left to the right diagonal while trotting, sit one beat on which you would normally rise. The rhythm thus becomes (on the left diagonal) *up-down*, *up-down* (then the change), *up-down-down*, and now (on the right diagonal), *up-down*, *up-down*.

THE SITTING TROT

At the *sitting trot* the rider sits deeply in the saddle and does not post. The sitting trot should be practiced at the slow trot only, since a fast trot is too springy to sit to on most horses. Be sure as you practice that you maintain good leg position and do not, through loss of balance, begin to grip with the backs of your legs. If this happens, return to the walk and adjust your position, then start the sitting trot again. Keep your hands as still as possible so you do not accidentally jerk on the horse's mouth with the reins. If you do find your hands jerking, slow the tempo until you can keep them still without difficulty.

TROTTING WITHOUT STIRRUPS

Trotting without stirrups can be good practice if done with care; it improves balance and helps the rider learn to *lengthen his or her leg* (bringing the leg farther down on the horse's side).

Remove both feet from the stirrup irons. Lift the irons up and cross the stirrup leathers over the horse's neck just in front of the withers. Place your legs correctly on the horse's sides as described in *The Overall Position*, page 82. Be sure that your calves remain lightly in contact with the horse's sides at all times, and that your heels remain lower than your toes.

Trotting without stirrups may be practiced at both the sitting and posting trots.

Posting and learning diagonals require practice. The process is rather like learning to ride a bicycle—you try and try, and just when you think you'll never learn it, you master it.

Learning to post, to tell which diagonal you are on, and to change diagonals at the trot can take several days for most riders. Don't be discouraged; everyone learns eventually, and once you have mastered these skills, you will wonder why they ever seemed difficult.

The Canter

The *canter* has three beats followed by a *moment of suspension* during which all four feet are off the ground. The three beats plus the moment of suspension make up a single stride, or pace, of the canter (see figure 47).

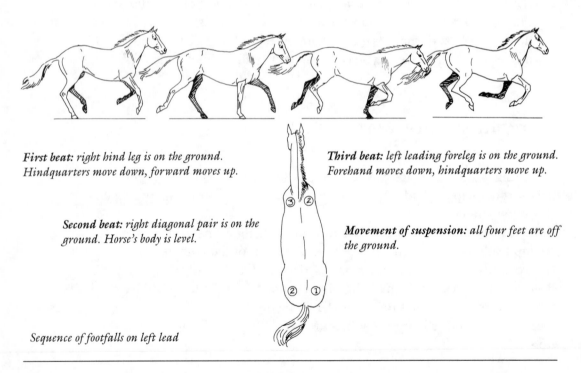

First beat: *right hind leg is on the ground. Hindquarters move down, forward moves up.*

Third beat: *left leading foreleg is on the ground. Forehand moves down, hindquarters move up.*

Second beat: *right diagonal pair is on the ground. Horse's body is level.*

Movement of suspension: *all four feet are off the ground.*

Sequence of footfalls on left lead

FIGURE 47: **The Canter on Left Lead**

During the canter, the horse *leads* with either his right or his left foreleg. The leading foreleg is so named because, when viewed from the side, it appears always to be slightly in advance of the other foreleg.

On left lead, the sequence of footfalls is as follows: right hind, right diagonal pair, left leading fore, followed by a moment of suspension. (The right diagonal pair consists of the right fore and the left hind, moving at the same time.)

A horse can go into the canter from a halt, a walk, a trot, or a gallop. The beginning rider should first learn to give the aids for the canter from the walk, and then from the trot.

It is easiest for a horse to turn in the direction of his leading foreleg. That is, when a horse is on left lead, it is easiest for him to turn to the left. The canter should be practiced on a circle about twenty-five feet in diameter, because turning toward the inside encourages the horse to take the inside lead. The terms *inside* and *outside* refer to the inside and the outside of the turn; going counterclockwise, the inside is the left side, and the outside is the right.

THE AIDS FOR THE CANTER ON LEFT LEAD: FROM THE WALK

The aids for the canter on left lead from a walk are as follows (see figure 48): Your inside (left) hand puts a slight, steady pressure on the inside rein. This hand moves backward on a diagonal line from the left side of the horse's

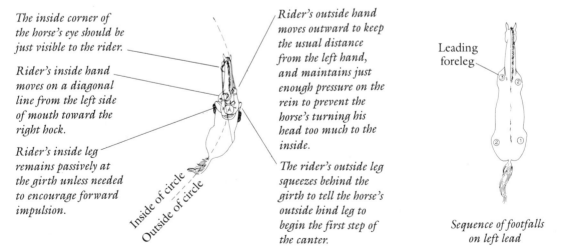

The inside corner of the horse's eye should be just visible to the rider.

Rider's inside hand moves on a diagonal line from the left side of mouth toward the right hock.

Rider's inside leg remains passively at the girth unless needed to encourage forward impulsion.

Inside of circle
Outside of circle

Rider's outside hand moves outward to keep the usual distance from the left hand, and maintains just enough pressure on the rein to prevent the horse's turning his head too much to the inside.

The rider's outside leg squeezes behind the girth to tell the horse's outside hind leg to begin the first step of the canter.

Leading foreleg

Sequence of footfalls on left lead

FIGURE 48:   *The Aids for the Canter on Left Lead*

mouth toward the right hock. This is called the *indirect rein*. Your outside (right) hand moves just enough to the outside to maintain the usual distance between your hands. This is a *supporting rein,* which prevents the horse's head from turning too much to the inside; you should be able to just see the corner of the horse's left eye.

As the horse points the toe of his left forefoot and touches it to the ground, give a squeeze with your outside (right) leg three or four inches behind the girth. This, combined with the rein aids, tells the horse to use his outside (right) hind leg to begin the first step of the canter rather than complete the step of the walk.

Allow your inside (left) leg to lie passively in its normal position at the girth unless needed to increase forward impulsion, in which case you should squeeze inward with your left calf at the girth, as necessary.

THE AIDS FOR THE CANTER ON LEFT LEAD: FROM THE TROT

The aids for the canter from the trot are the same as those from the walk (indirect inside rein, supporting outside rein, outside leg behind the girth, inside leg passive at the girth). What is different is the *moment* at which you give the aids.

To canter on left lead, first trot on a circle about twenty-five feet in diameter in a counterclockwise direction. Post on the outside diagonal: as the right shoulder goes forward, you rise, and as it comes back, you sit.

Place a slight steady pressure on the inside (left) rein and just enough pressure on the outside (right) rein to limit the bend in the horse's neck so that the corner of his left eye is barely visible. Keep this pressure constant. Do not allow the horse to increase the speed of the trot. If he attempts to, steady him with equal, gentle pressure on both reins.

During the second beat of the trot squeeze your outside (right) leg three or four inches behind the girth as you sit. This tells the horse to begin the first beat of the canter with his right hind leg instead of beginning a new step of the trot. If the horse breaks correctly into a canter, cease giving the aids and assume the correct position at the canter (see *The Position of the Rider at the Canter,* below).

If the horse merely trots faster, regain the slow trot; repeat the aids, using the whip behind your outside leg, if necessary; and increase the pressure on both reins slightly.

THE POSITION OF THE RIDER AT THE CANTER

The horse's back moves with a rocking motion during the canter (see figure 47, page 110). On the first beat of the canter the outside hind leg treads well under his body; at this stage, his hindquarters are lower than his forehand (the front half of the horse). On the second beat,

As horse lowers and extends neck and raises croup, rider sits upright. As horse raises neck and lowers croup, rider inclines forward. Hands remain still relative to the horse's withers. The angle of the elbows opens and closes noticeably.

FIGURE 49:   *At the Canter*

the outside diagonal pair (outside fore, inside hind) carries his body forward; at this stage, his hindquarters and forehand are level. On the third beat, the leading foreleg supports his body; at the end of this beat, his forehand is lower than his hindquarters. During the moment of suspension, the hindquarters again reach under the horse's body and the sequence begins again.

You must counteract this seesaw motion—first one end of the horse rocking up, then the other—with your own body position (see figure 49). To do so, allow the angle of your hip to open and close with each stride. Your back should remain straight; only the angle of your hip must change.

As the horse strikes off into the canter from a walk, close the angle of your hip, inclining your body slightly forward relative to the horse's back. On the second beat, sit nearly upright. On the third beat, sit upright. During the moment of suspension, begin to incline forward once again in preparation for the first beat of the canter. In fact, your position relative to the ground remains the same; it changes only relative to the horse, who is seesawing beneath you.

THE FLYING CHANGE OF LEADS

A horse is capable of doing a *flying change of leads* at any time he chooses during the canter. In the flying change, the horse switches to the opposite lead during the moment of suspension. If he does a flying change from left lead to right, he rearranges his legs during the moment of suspension so that the following stride of the canter will begin not with the right hind leg, as before, but rather with the left hind leg, thus initiating a canter stride on right lead. The sequence then becomes: left hind, left diagonal pair, right leading fore.

If the horse changes leads *only* in front or behind, but continues to move the other two legs as before, the canter is *disunited*. (This is also called *cross cantering*.) This is a serious fault and should always be corrected without delay by bringing the horse momentarily to a trot and giving the aids for the correct lead.

In advanced work, the horse can be taught to do a flying change on command, but an unasked-for flying change should be corrected in the same way as a disunited canter. The only exception to this occurs when the rider crosses natural terrain, such as hills or fields. Here the horse should be allowed to change leads at will as terrain dictates; if forced to remain on one lead when he needs to change leads to maintain his balance on uneven ground, the horse may stumble.

TO GO FROM THE CANTER INTO THE TROT OR WALK

Move your hands slightly forward momentarily so as to remove the light contact you have had with the horse's mouth; this warns him that you are going to give the aids for the trot or walk. Then, during the moment of suspension, use both your rein and leg aids just as you would to go from a walk into a halt (see *The Aids for the Halt*, page 117). At first, go from a canter into a trot for a stride or two, and then go into a walk. Later, as your skill in giving the aids and following the horse's movement develops, you will be able to go from a canter directly into a walk. Keep in mind, however, that the latter puts strain on the horse's legs, and use the transition from canter to trot most of the time.

The Gallop

At the *gallop* a racehorse can reach speeds of forty miles per hour. The gallop is not merely a fast canter. The sequence of footfalls changes slightly: it has four beats, not three as in the canter.

When a horse moves from a canter into a gallop, the second beat of the canter (the outside diagonal pair) breaks up into two distinct beats, with the hind leg moving slightly sooner than the foreleg. The sequence, on left lead, thus becomes: right hind, left hind, right fore, left (leading) fore, followed by a moment of suspension. At the gallop, the horse's body rocks much less than at the canter; the gallop, being "flatter," is actually much easier to sit to than the canter on most horses.

The Hand Gallop

The *hand gallop*, which is often required by horse show judges as a test of contestants' control of their mounts, is not a true gallop but a fast canter "in hand"; that is, the horse is in control and the rider can stop him at will. The hand gallop has three beats, like the canter.

THE AIDS FOR THE HAND GALLOP

To hand gallop, simply transfer most of your weight to your heels so your seat is not actually sitting in the saddle but rather hovers slightly above it, and lean forward slightly more than you would at the trot. Urge the horse into a faster canter with your calves, maintaining light contact with the reins. Keep the rhythm steady; if you feel the horse begin to gain too much speed, put enough pressure on the reins to maintain a steady rhythm.

The true four-beat gallop is too fast to perform safely under most conditions because a single false step can break a horse's leg. A horse will seldom gallop of his own will unless he perceives life-threatening danger and panics and bolts. If a horse bolts, it can be frightening unless you know how to stop him (see chapter 11).

Bolting

Bolting is running at full speed, at a flat-out gallop, often in a panic. Do not create situations that will encourage a horse to break into a true gallop. For example, never canter toward the barn at the end of a ride, but walk the last part of the way home. Do not race with other horses who canter alongside your horse, but give your horse the aids to slow down when you first feel him pick up speed in company.

The Halt

The *halt* occurs when the horse entirely stops the movement of all four feet. Ideally, the horse should halt squarely, standing flat on the ground with weight distributed equally on all four feet. At first, practice the halt from a walk, later from a trot. Halting from a canter or hand gallop is possible, but if done too often it strains the horse's legs and can cause lameness or permanent injury.

THE AIDS FOR THE HALT

To go from a walk to a halt, tighten both your calves exactly as you would to move forward from the halt into a walk. At the same time, bring your elbows back an inch or two, thereby putting a gentle but definite pressure on both reins equally. Do not look down. Do not bend your wrists or twist your fingers. Do not change your body position. The instant the horse halts, stop giving all aids: move your hands forward enough to create slack in the reins, and cease your calves' signal.

If the horse continues to walk for more than a second or two after you have given the aids to halt, give the aids again, using stronger, more obvious rein pressure and a definite squeeze with your legs. Do not yank or jerk the reins; *merely apply enough pressure to get a response and wait for the horse to stop.* If you have to apply fairly strong pressure on the reins, be especially aware of the moment the horse halts and reward him immediately by ceasing all pressure on the reins and from your legs. It is sometimes difficult to remember to stop giving the aids in this situation, because you may unconsciously think, "If it took this much pressure on the reins to make the horse halt, I'd better not relax the reins now that he has stopped, or he'll just start walking again." Do not give in to this way of thinking. *When the horse stops, always release.* This is his reward for stopping. If the pressure on the reins remains after he has halted, there will be no incentive for him to halt, and he will quickly learn to ignore you. Most horses with so-called "hard" mouths are simply horses who have learned that no matter what they do, their riders still pull on the reins. Eventually they ignore their riders.

When learning to halt, remember to use your legs to the same degree that you use your reins. Your legs "speak" to the horse's hind legs by telling the horse to use them. He therefore brings them under his body and halts properly balanced (see figure 50a). If the horse fails to do this when he halts, he will halt "strung out"—unbalanced and with one hind foot trailing behind.

Note that to halt, you must not *pull* on the reins (see figure 50b). Pulling means giving a strong tug that increases, then decreases (usually because your arms get tired), then increases again, then tapers off, and so forth, without regard as to whether or not the horse has obeyed. The essential point is that you must not let the pressure on the reins decrease while the horse is pulling

A

Correct: *Rider drives horse's hind legs under him, applies pressure equally on both reins, and horse halts balanced and square. Rider ceases to give pressure. Horse stands on slack rein.*

B

Incorrect: *Rider fails to use legs, pulls on the reins, eases off, pulls again, eases off before horse has halted. Horse pulls back against the rider, halts unbalanced.*

FIGURE 50:   *The Halt*

against the reins and resisting; the pressure must *only* cease, and cease completely, at the moment the horse comes to a complete halt. Therefore, you must apply rein pressure strongly enough that the horse wants to do something to get rid of it. You must not lessen this pressure in any way until the horse has halted completely. When he has, reward him by ceasing the aids smoothly, instantly, and completely.

Turns and Circles

A *turn* is part of a circle. In all turns and circles, it is important that the horse's backbone, from ears to tail, be curved in the same direction and to the same degree as the turn or circle. The bend of the horse must be neither more nor less than that of the turn. To ask the horse to turn, and to create the proper curve in his backbone, the rider uses both rein and leg aids.

Inside refers to the inside of the turn or circle. On a clockwise turn, the inside hand and leg are the right; the outside the left.

The aids for turning are the same whether the horse is walking, trotting, or cantering.

There are two kinds of turns that the beginning rider should know how to use: the *direct rein turn* and the *indirect rein turn*.

THE DIRECT REIN TURN

The *direct rein turn*, sometimes called the *opening rein*, is the simplest turn, and is so named because the rein moves in the same direction that the rider wants the horse to turn. It does not slow the horse's speed and can be used to make the horse move on a smaller circle than he was originally on.

THE DIRECT REIN TURN TO THE RIGHT

The rein aids for the direct rein turn to the right are as follows: Move your right hand to the right, a few inches away from the horse's neck, being careful to move it only sideways, not backward. At the same time, move your left hand forward an inch or two to allow the horse's head and neck to turn toward the right. When the horse has turned as much as you wish, bring your hands back to their normal position (see figure 51).

A beginning rider should practice direct rein turns in this way, until the use of the rein aids is automatic, then add the leg aids, which must be simultaneous with the rein aids in order to make a correct turn.

For a turn to the right, the leg aids are as follows: The right (inside) leg remains in the normal position at the girth to maintain impulsion forward. That is, if the horse slows down during the turn, the inside leg squeezes to remind the horse to move forward at a steady rhythm.

The left (outside) leg moves to a position three or four inches behind the girth. If needed, it tells the outside hind leg, by means of a squeeze, not to swing outward (that is, not to move too far to the left) on the turn. The rider

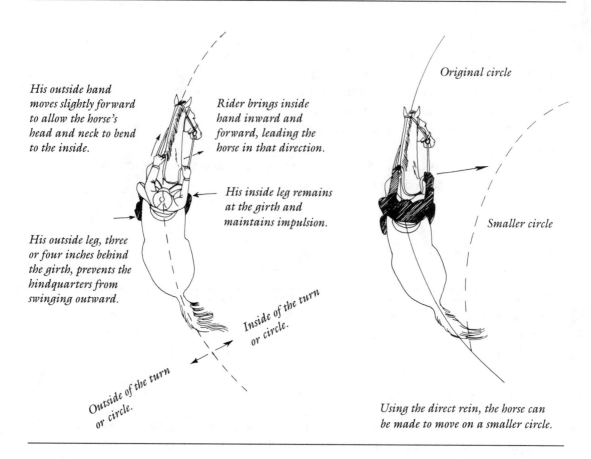

His outside hand moves slightly forward to allow the horse's head and neck to bend to the inside.

Rider brings inside hand inward and forward, leading the horse in that direction.

His inside leg remains at the girth and maintains impulsion.

His outside leg, three or four inches behind the girth, prevents the hindquarters from swinging outward.

Inside of the turn or circle.

Outside of the turn or circle.

Original circle

Smaller circle

Using the direct rein, the horse can be made to move on a smaller circle.

FIGURE 51:   *The Direct Rein Turn*

thus controls both the horse's forward movement and the curve of his backbone so that they conform to the curve of the turn.

Two points are of particular importance. First, during a turn, the curve must be gradual enough that the horse's backbone is able to conform to it, not only in the neck, which is very flexible, but also in the less-flexible part of the backbone that extends from the saddle to the horse's tail. If the turn is too sharp and the horse is unable to curve the latter part of his backbone to conform to it, he will simply swing his hindquarters out on the turn. For this reason you should make all turns and circles no less than twenty feet in diameter until the horse learns, through practice, to bend easily. (This can take many months.)

Second, you must pay attention to the rhythm of the horse's gait, and not allow it to slow or speed up during a turn. The horse's rhythm must remain

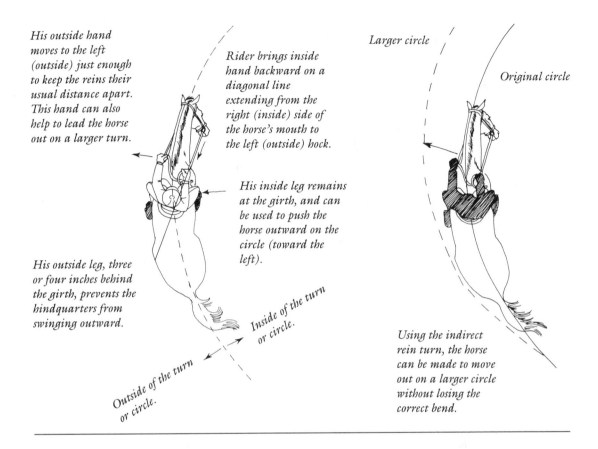

His outside hand moves to the left (outside) just enough to keep the reins their usual distance apart. This hand can also help to lead the horse out on a larger turn.

Rider brings inside hand backward on a diagonal line extending from the right (inside) side of the horse's mouth to the left (outside) hock.

Larger circle

Original circle

His inside leg remains at the girth, and can be used to push the horse outward on the circle (toward the left).

His outside leg, three or four inches behind the girth, prevents the hindquarters from swinging outward.

Inside of the turn or circle.

Outside of the turn or circle.

Using the indirect rein turn, the horse can be made to move out on a larger circle without losing the correct bend.

FIGURE 52: *The Indirect Rein Turn*

steady and regular throughout the turn. To maintain steady rhythm, use the same aids you would for the halt (if you want to slow down) or for going from the halt to the walk (if you want to increase the tempo); however, use them *only enough* to maintain the rhythm.

THE INDIRECT REIN TURN

The *indirect rein turn* tends to slow the horse's forward movement. It therefore can be used to steady the pace of a horse who wants to speed up during a turn. It can also be used to move the horse out on a larger turn or circle while maintaining the correct bend (see figure 52).

THE INDIRECT REIN TURN TO THE RIGHT

The aids for an indirect rein turn to the right are as follows: Your right (inside) hand comes back at an angle, putting a slight, steady pressure on the rein. This hand moves on a diagonal line that extends from the right side of the horse's mouth toward the left hock without crossing the horse's neck. The reins must be short enough so that your right hand comes no farther back than the horse's withers, or preferably remains slightly in front of the withers.

At the same time, your left (outside) hand moves to the left, away from the horse's neck, just enough to keep the hands their usual distance—about ten inches—apart. The outside hand can be used passively or actively.

If used passively, the outside hand simply limits the amount of bend in the horse's neck. That is, if the horse attempts to turn his head too far to the right, the left rein resists him.

If used actively, the outside hand can move the horse out on a larger circle. When used in this way, the outside hand gives an active squeeze on the rein to the left, leading the horse outward, and releasing the pressure on the rein momentarily when the horse responds correctly. This hand then asks again for the next response, until step by step the larger circle is achieved. At the same time, however, the inside hand must continue to keep the horse curved to conform to the circle.

While the reins are being used, the legs must simultaneously give the correct aids. Your inside leg may either remain passively at the girth, or be used to support the outside hand in moving the horse outward on a turn. If used actively, it squeezes in the same rhythm as the outside hand.

Your outside leg, used slightly behind the girth, prevents the horse from swinging his hindquarters to the left. Unless needed, this leg remains passive. Give an active squeeze a few inches behind the girth with your outside leg only if the horse swings his hindquarters out on the turn.

The Reinback

I n the *reinback* (backing up), the horse's legs move in diagonal pairs exactly as in the trot, but in a reverse direction. When each diagonal pair has moved once, a single step of the reinback is complete.

The aids for the reinback are as follows: Put gentle, steady pressure on both reins. Then immediately give the leg aids for walking forward. The pressure on both reins prevents the horse from moving in a forward direction. When the horse moves one diagonal pair backward, soften the pressure on the reins and cease the leg aids momentarily; then immediately ask for the other diagonal pair to move.

Do not *pull* the reins—that is, do not increase and decrease the pressure arbitrarily. Rather, create forward movement with your legs while preventing the horse, by steady pressure on the reins, from using this energy to actually move forward.

Be sure to reward the movement of each diagonal pair; otherwise the horse will learn to hurry backward for an indeterminate number of steps and you will be unable to obtain a specific number of backward steps. This could have unfortunate consequences if you find yourself on a trail in *trappy* country (very uneven terrain) where you can back up only so far to get around an obstacle without backing off a piece of uneven ground.

QUIZ

1. Sequence of footfalls at the walk is
   - (A) left hind, right hind, left fore, right fore
   - (B) left hind, left fore, right hind, right fore
   - (C) left hind, left fore and right hind together, right fore

2. Sequence of footfalls at the trot is
   - (A) left hind and left fore together, then right hind and right fore together
   - (B) left hind and right fore together, then right hind and left fore together
   - (C) left and right hind together, then left and right fore together

3. Sequence of footfalls at the canter on left lead is
   - (A) left hind, left diagonal pair, right fore
   - (B) left fore, left diagonal pair, right hind
   - (C) right hind, right diagonal pair, left fore

4. Turning to the right, the horse will prefer to canter on
   - (A) right lead
   - (B) left lead
   - (C) neither; both are equally convenient

5. *True or false:* A gallop is actually nothing but a very fast canter.

6. Another name for posting is
   - (A) extended trot
   - (B) trot rising
   - (C) sitting trot

7. During the reinback, the rider should
   - (A) release the reins briefly as each diagonal pair moves
   - (B) release the reins only after the horse has completed the required number of steps
   - (C) use reins only, not legs, to give the aids

8. In turns, the horse must
   - (A) bend his head and neck in the same direction he is going
   - (B) bend slightly the opposite way from the direction he is going
   - (C) bend his entire backbone from head to tail to the same degree as the turn

9. The turn that tends to slow the forward movement of the horse is the
   - (A) direct rein turn
   - (B) indirect rein turn
   - (C) volte turn

10. If the horse cuts in on a turn, making it too small, the rider should use the aids for the
    - (A) direct rein turn
    - (B) indirect rein turn
    - (C) neither of the above

Under guidance of a riding instructor, perform the following mounted tests of your progress:

1. Ride away from a group of other mounted riders. Do this at a walk, trot, and canter. Walk back to the group; do not allow the horse to trot or canter back.

2. Stay behind while a group of riders rides on ahead of you. If your horse fidgets and becomes restless, walk him in a small circle, but do not allow him to join the other horses until you decide to do so.

3. Ride past an open gate; do not allow the horse to exit as he goes by it at a walk, trot, and canter.

4. Set up a slalom course of poles or bricks and zigzag through it, first at a walk and then at a trot.

5. Canter the horse on right lead from a walk and a trot. Repeat on left lead.

6. Canter ahead of a group of horses who are walking or trotting, then walk back.

7. Cross your stirrup irons in front of the saddle; walk, trot, and canter without losing your position or balance.

8. Without looking down, by feel alone, count out the beats at the walk.

9. Repeat at the trot.

10. Repeat at the canter.

11. Reinback four complete steps, walk forward six steps, reinback two steps, walk forward six steps, halt.

10

Cavalletti and Jumping

Jumping

The rider should learn how to jump under the guidance of an instructor, never alone. A hard hat should always be worn.

THE RIDER'S POSITION WHEN JUMPING

In going over a jump (also called a fence), a horse's center of gravity changes dynamically from well behind his middle point to well forward of it. During takeoff, as the horse pushes off the ground with his hind legs, propelling his forehand into the air, his center of gravity is to the rear. During the height of the jump his center of gravity moves to the middle. It moves forward as the horse lands on a single forefoot. The rider must modify his or her position in the saddle to remain in balance with the horse's center of gravity (see figure 53).

The angles of the hip, ankle, and elbow are of prime importance in jumping; each of these angles opens and closes noticeably. To a lesser degree, the angle of the knee also changes.

To allow each of these angles to become more or less acute as necessary,

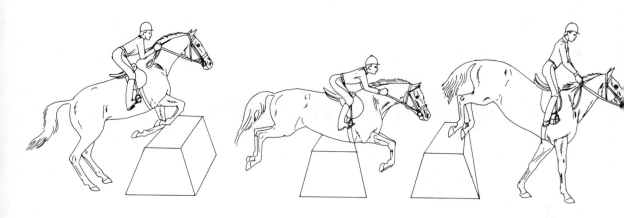

A
During take-off, angles of the elbows close, angles of knees open.

B
During flight phase, hip angle remains closed, elbow angles open as necessary to follow the movement of the horse's head forward and downward. Rider's back is nearly parallel to the ground.

C
On landing, angles of the rider's hips, elbows, and knees open; ankle joints close, absorbing shock of landing.

How the rider's position changes during the jump to remain at equilibrium with the horse's changing center of gravity.

FIGURE 53:   *Rider's Position Over a Jump*

shorten your stirrups two or three holes. Push your heels down and forward three or four inches so that the leathers hang slightly in front of the vertical. Close the angle of your hip so your waist is brought forward and your seat moves back. Your seat now hovers just above the seat of the saddle, barely touching, as your weight is pushed down into your heels. Do not let your back hunch; keep it straight or very slightly arched (see figure 54).

THE HORSE'S POSITION WHEN JUMPING

Ideally a horse should form a uniform arc over the fence. His backbone, including head and neck, should be curved to conform to the arc. This is called a *bascule,* and the horse is said to "use himself" over the fence.

His body should clear the obstacle by as small a margin as possible. His front and hind legs should tuck up well under his body; if his legs dangle, he must expend more energy to hoist his body higher into the air than if he folds his legs tightly against his body.

A horse will usually take off in front of the fence from a distance approximately equal to its height. For example, when approaching a three-foot jump, the horse will take off about three feet in front of it and land three

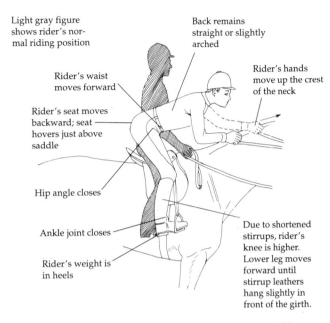

Light gray figure shows rider's normal riding position

Back remains straight or slightly arched

Rider's waist moves forward

Rider's hands move up the crest of the neck

Rider's seat moves backward; seat hovers just above saddle

Hip angle closes

Ankle joint closes

Rider's weight is in heels

Due to shortened stirrups, rider's knee is higher. Lower leg moves forward until stirrup leathers hang slightly in front of the girth.

Modification of the rider's seat for jumping position of rider during last three strides approaching a jump.

FIGURE 54: ***Getting into Jumping Position***

feet after it. If he is traveling faster, he will take off sooner, adding as much as fifty percent to the takeoff distance. That is, he might take off as much as four and one-half feet in front of the jump and land four and one-half feet after it.

The horse also looks at the *ground line* (the base line, usually marked by a pole on the ground) of a fence to judge his takeoff. He can judge more easily if the ground line is clearly marked at the base of the jump with a pole. A horse will take off earlier if the ground line is moved out from the jump; this is a useful practice when correcting a horse who makes too tight an arc over an upright fence.

Solid fences are easier for horses to judge than those they can see through, but both horse and rider should learn to jump all sorts of obstacles—both inviting ones and odd-looking ones—from the start. Do not avoid jumping certain kinds of fences for fear that the horse will *refuse* (stop just before the fence) because they are strange-looking. Rather, set up a wide variety of fences, preferably solid ones that cannot be knocked down (so the horse learns to respect them), at heights not exceeding two feet six inches, and familiarize both yourself and the horse with jumping them. Then very gradually increase their height so neither horse nor rider is *overfaced* (intimidated) by a fence that seems too high to be safely jumped.

Cavalletti

Cavalletti are used as the first stage of jumping for both horse and rider (see figure 55). The word *cavalletti* (singular *cavalletto*) is Italian for "little horses," which is what these small jumps look like. The Italians, the first proponents of the forward seat now universally used in jumping, invented and developed the use of cavalletti.

Cavalletti are poles about ten feet long, usually with the corners beveled to form an octagonal shape. Attached to each end of the pole is a sturdy wooden X-shaped support that holds the pole ten, fifteen, or twenty inches above the ground, depending upon which way the pole is turned (see figure 55c).

Use of cavalletti helps the rider develop good form over fences and teaches the ability to judge the horse's stride coming into a fence and moving between fences. It helps develop the horse physically; it lets him learn to judge his own

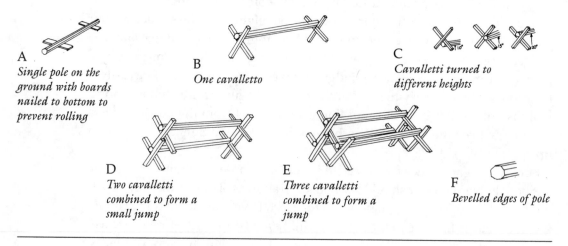

A
Single pole on the ground with boards nailed to bottom to prevent rolling

B
One cavalletto

C
Cavalletti turned to different heights

D
Two cavalletti combined to form a small jump

E
Three cavalletti combined to form a jump

F
Bevelled edges of pole

FIGURE 55: *Cavalletti*

stride and use his hindquarters properly in jumping. It encourages a horse to learn that jumping is all in a day's work and nothing to get excited about. Many horses become excited when being ridden toward a fence because their training in jumping has been hurried or their experiences traumatic. They may have been jabbed in the mouth by an inexperienced rider while jumping; or had their reins pulled just before the moment of takeoff, when concentration is needed most; or been made to jump fences too large for their level of training; or fallen into or over a fence and consequently lost courage. In an effort to run away from such problems, these horses rush their fences, and become "hot," or agitated, if asked to jump. Cavalletti can restore confidence to both horses and riders who have had bad experiences in jumping.

Cavalletti should be set up in an enclosed area such as a ring, indoor arena, or quiet field away from distractions. When using cavalletti be sure to pull your stirrup irons up two or three holes, and to hold your reins three or four inches shorter than you would for ordinary riding.

Begin by walking the horse on a straight line over a single pole lying on the ground. (A small piece of board nailed to each end will prevent it from rolling if the horse accidentally touches it (see figure 55a). As you approach the pole, modify your riding position into the jumping position. Be sure to keep your backbone upright above the horse's; do not lean over to one side. For the last eighteen feet before crossing the pole, move your hands up the crest of the horse's neck, allowing him to extend and lower his head and neck as much as he wants to. If he attempts to wander off the straight line toward the pole, use direct rein to keep him straight. Turn after crossing the pole, and repeat the exercise ten or twenty times, alternating directions (see figure 56a).

Next, trot over the pole. Proceed as shown in figure 56, performing exercises A through J one at a time. If the horse shows any tendency to rush, go back to the previous step and repeat the exercise until he is perfectly calm. In the exercises at a canter, you can make the horse take the correct lead after the jump by using direct rein in midair as he jumps. That is, to make the horse take left lead after the fence, use left direct rein in midair.

As the horse takes off, be sure that your own body, from hips to head, does not lean to one side, but that your backbone is aligned with the horse's.

If you feel any loss of balance when jumping at the trot or canter, grasp a handful of mane with one hand just before takeoff. It is better to hold the mane than to use a neck strap as the latter may slip sideways or too far back toward

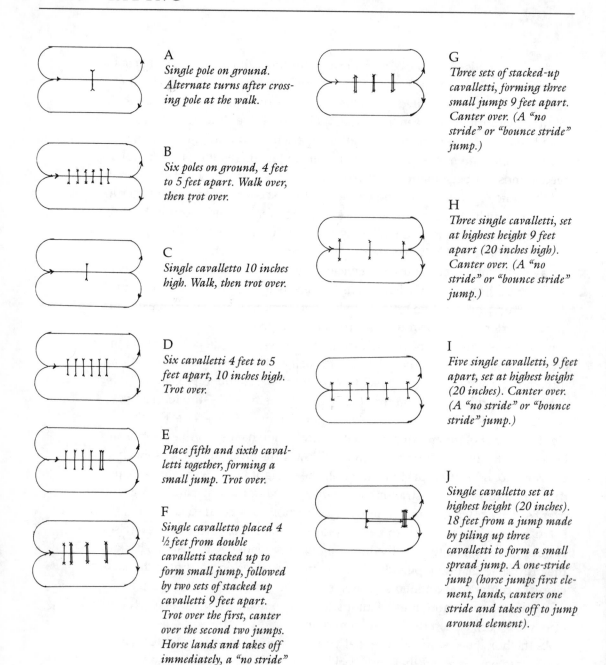

A

Single pole on ground. Alternate turns after crossing pole at the walk.

B

Six poles on ground, 4 feet to 5 feet apart. Walk over, then trot over.

C

Single cavalletto 10 inches high. Walk, then trot over.

D

Six cavalletti 4 feet to 5 feet apart, 10 inches high. Trot over.

E

Place fifth and sixth cavalletti together, forming a small jump. Trot over.

F

Single cavalletto placed 4 ½ feet from double cavalletti stacked up to form small jump, followed by two sets of stacked up cavalletti 9 feet apart. Trot over the first, canter over the second two jumps. Horse lands and takes off immediately, a "no stride" or "bounce stride" jump.

G

Three sets of stacked-up cavalletti, forming three small jumps 9 feet apart. Canter over. (A "no stride" or "bounce stride" jump.)

H

Three single cavalletti, set at highest height 9 feet apart (20 inches high). Canter over. (A "no stride" or "bounce stride" jump.)

I

Five single cavalletti, 9 feet apart, set at highest height (20 inches). Canter over. (A "no stride" or "bounce stride" jump.)

J

Single cavalletto set at highest height (20 inches). 18 feet from a jump made by piling up three cavalletti to form a small spread jump. A one-stride jump (horse jumps first element, lands, canters one stride and takes off to jump around element).

FIGURE 56:   ***Stages in Use of Cavalletti***

you to allow you to keep your hands properly placed. Never give the horse an accidental jab in the mouth or you will quickly discourage him from jumping. It is unlikely that you will make this serious error if you hold the mane until your jumping position is firmly established. However, if despite all efforts you find that your weight has fallen behind the horse's movement, and you have been *left behind* (thrown backward) as he jumps, let the reins slip through your fingers rather than jab him in the mouth.

Kinds of Jumps

J umps are generally eight to ten feet in length. The fence itself is held in place at each end by vertical supports called *standards*, to which are attached holders called *cups*; the cups can be moved up or down to adjust the height of the jump. There are two basic types of jumps: *upright* and *spread* (see figure 57).

Upright jumps are no more than a few inches wide and consist of single pairs of standards along with the rail or rails they support. Common kinds of upright fences include gates, post-and-rails, picket fences, and painted poles.

Spread jumps can vary in depth from one to several feet and include jumps made from two or more pairs of standards that support parallel poles, called *oxers*; *chicken coops* (triangular, solid wooden jumps); *walls* (jumps made of wood painted to resemble brick or stone); *ditches* (trenches filled with water that is either real or simulated by securing a sheet of shiny plastic to the ground); piled-up telephone poles; and so forth.

Jumping puts a strain on the horse's legs and feet, and if done too often can cause lameness and a sour attitude in the horse. Unlike the jumping of cavalletti, which are low and can be jumped daily without harm as long as the ground is not dry and hard, the jumping of fences of two feet six inches and higher should be carried out with discretion. If is far better to jump twenty two-foot-high fences well, twice a week, than to jump twice that number poorly, several days a week.

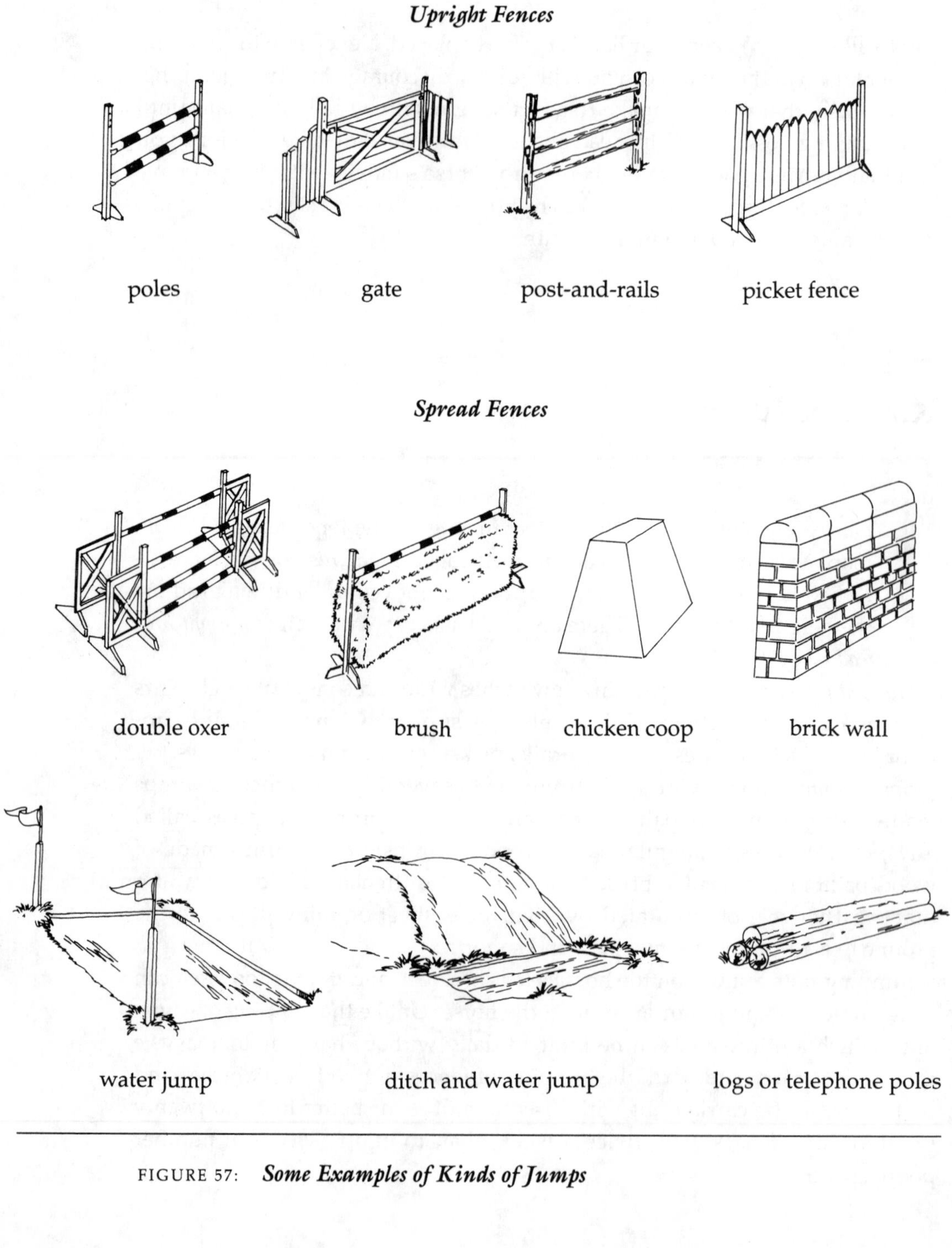

Upright Fences

poles   gate   post-and-rails   picket fence

Spread Fences

double oxer   brush   chicken coop   brick wall

water jump   ditch and water jump   logs or telephone poles

FIGURE 57:   *Some Examples of Kinds of Jumps*

Never ask a horse to jump any fence you are not absolutely certain both you and he are capable of jumping. Take into account the horse's level of training, his physical development, the condition of the ground (avoid jumping on muddy, icy, or slippery ground), and your own experience. Practice over low fences, and increase their height gradually over a period of weeks or months.

Runouts

A *runout* occurs when a horse approaches a fence he is meant to jump, but avoids by ducking out to one side. To prevent runouts, ride straight toward the center of the fence, maintaining light contact with the horse's mouth during the approach. Correct, as soon as you feel it, any attempt by the horse to deviate from a straight approach. Use direct rein and the opposite leg; for example, if the horse attempts to run out to the right, use left direct rein (move your left hand to the left) and your right leg to push his body to the left. If necessary, use the whip in the right hand to reinforce your right leg.

If, despite your efforts to correct a runout in its early stages, the horse succeeds, you must stop him as soon as possible, hold him still with the reins in one hand, and give him three or four sharp swats beside your leg with the whip with the other. Punish on the same side as the runout; if the horse ran out to the right, use the whip on his right side, encouraging him to move away from the whip and toward the jump. If a horse has a known tendency to run out to one side, always carry the whip in that hand.

Once a horse learns to jump fences in the center of the fence, straight-on without running out, he should be ridden over fences approached from other angles as well. Keep the angle slight at first, and increase it somewhat as he gains experience.

Refusals

A *refusal* occurs when a horse stops short in front of a jump and refuses to go over it. When a horse "quits," punishment must be swift and the jump must be gotten over as soon as possible after the punishment.

Punishment for a refusal differs from that for a runout because a refusal usually leaves the horse standing near the jump and facing it. Punishment at that moment might prompt the horse to attempt to jump from a standstill, which is difficult for the rider to stay with and which may be impossible for the horse to do successfully—he could land in the middle of the fence.

Therefore, *back* the horse five or six steps from the fence; then hold him on the spot with the reins in one hand, administer three or four good swats on his sides behind both of your legs with the whip, and allow him to trot or canter over the fence immediately.

The key to preventing refusals is to ride the horse actively forward. This does not mean riding *fast*, but rather being sure that he moves forward willingly at an alert, steady pace in response to squeezes from your leg. If you feel him hesitate as you approach the jump, do not wait for him to refuse; use your whip instantly so that the hesitation never becomes a refusal.

Rushing

When a horse approaches a fence too hurriedly and excitedly, he is *rushing* it. If he can be steadied by applying firm pressure on the reins, do so; but if pressure on the reins merely upsets him more, go back to the previous stage of training. For instance, if he rushes over small fences, go back to cavalletti; if he rushes over cavalletti, go back to a single pole on the ground.

Two exercises can be useful: *circling* and the *line stop*. In the former exercise, if a horse shows any tendency to rush as you approach the fence, simply turn off to one side or the other as soon as he begins to rush, instead of jumping the fence, and ride a circle about thirty feet in diameter. Repeat until the horse makes an absolutely calm approach. Only jump a fence if the horse shows no tendency to hurry.

In a *line stop*, maintain very light contact with the horse's mouth and let him rush as much as he wants *before* the fence, then stop him abruptly on the far side. He will soon learn to anticipate the stop and slow down before the fence.

1. The word *cavalletti* means
   (A) small jumps
   (B) little horses
   (C) practice jumps

2. Horses who rush their fences should
   (A) be allowed to rush; they'll get over it in time
   (B) be taken over the biggest fence they are capable of jumping to tire them out
   (C) be trained slowly using cavalletti, going back to the previous step of training at the first sign of rushing

3. *True or false:* Cavalletti can be turned so that they are ten, fifteen, or twenty inches from the ground.

4. *True or false:* The rider's form when using cavalletti should be identical to that used for jumping regular fences.

5. When jumping, a horse judges his takeoff point by focusing on
   (A) the groundline of the fence
   (B) the top of the fence
   (C) both of the above

6. A horse jumping from a slow canter will probably take off and land
   (A) farther from the fence than if he were traveling at a fast canter
   (B) closer to the fence than if he were traveling at a fast canter

7. For most horses traveling at the trot, cavalletti should be spaced approximately how far apart?
   (A) two feet
   (B) four to four and one-half feet
   (C) six and one-half to seven feet

8. Most horses can canter over cavalletti most easily if they are spaced apart
   (A) six feet
   (B) nine to ten feet
   (C) sixteen feet

9. *True or false:* To influence the horse to take the left lead at the canter when he lands after a jump, the rider should use left direct rein when the horse is in the air over the jump.

10. *True or false:* Runouts and refusals should be corrected in exactly the same way.

Perform the following mounted tests:

1. Trot over six cavalletti.

2. Canter over three cavalletti; stop on a straight line after the last cavalletto.

3. Jump an upright fence three feet high.

4. Jump a spread jump three feet high and three feet wide.

5. Jump a two-foot fence with good form without using stirrups.

6. Canter over the same jump at a slow canter and a fast canter, after each time placing a small stick on the ground to mark the place where you think the horse will take off.

Answers: 1B, 2C, 3. true. 4. true. 5C, 6B, 7B, 8B, 9. true. 10. false.

11

Care of Horse and Equipment

Grooming

Grooming benefits the horse in several ways. It stimulates circulation, activates oil glands in the skin, removes dead skin and shedding hair, and improves the appearance of the horse's coat. It also gives you a chance to be sure that no cuts, swelling, scrapes, or bruises go undetected, particularly on parts of the head or body—such as the girth area or the poll—where they could be irritated by tack.

The minimum amount of grooming necessary before riding consists of knocking off obvious caked dirt or manure with a curry comb, brushing the hair with a body brush, washing off stubborn stains with a sponge, picking out the feet with a hoof pick, and removing hay and straw from the mane and tail (see figure 58). Be sure areas where the saddle and girth will touch are smooth, clean, and free of cuts or scrapes.

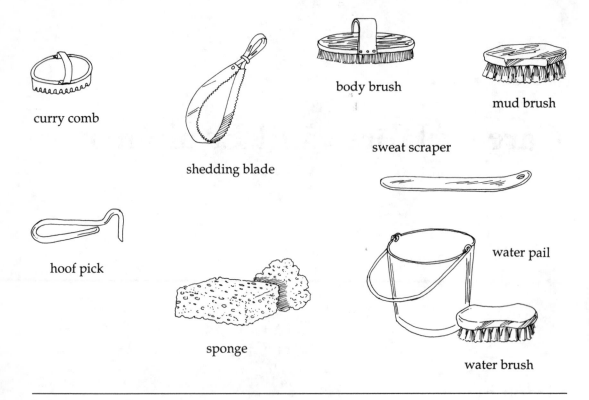

curry comb

shedding blade

body brush

sweat scraper

mud brush

hoof pick

sponge

water pail

water brush

FIGURE 58:   *Grooming Tools*

AFTER RIDING

A thorough grooming should be performed when the horse is returned to the stable; after exercise, the pores of his skin will have brought dirt to the surface. Note, however, that a horse must always be cooled out completely before he is returned to the stable. Test between the front legs and on the chest with your hand; if there is any sign of dampness, walk him until he is dry and the same temperature all over.

Tie the horse up before grooming so he does not move around. Use cross ties, or tie him in his stall with a halter and the quick-release knot shown in figure 59. Use only a soft brush, not a curry comb, on his head and from the knees and hocks down. Do not use a brush on the tail, as it will pull the hairs out. Rather, separate the strands by hand a few at a time.

Wipe the horse's face, ears, nose, and eyes with a damp sponge. Curry the body vigorously with a curry comb (the rubber ones are better than those of metal, which can scratch), using a circular motion. Brush out dirt with a body brush, using short, vigorous strokes. Put your back into both currying and brushing; listless dabs are of no benefit. Look for signs of swelling and irritation, particularly in the areas of the girth and saddle. A horse with swollen areas or open galls must not be ridden. The tack should be examined for dirt and the cause of irritation eliminated.

Pick out the horse's feet with a hoof pick. To do this, stand op-

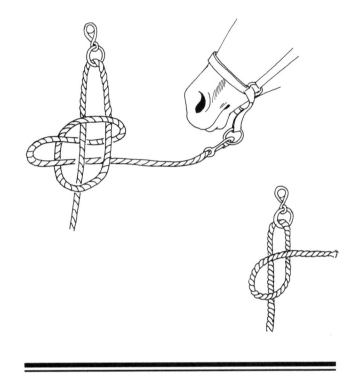

FIGURE 59:   *The Quick Release Knot*

posite the left shoulder, facing the tail. Lean your shoulder against the horse's, slide your hand down the cannon bone to the fetlock, say "Come up," and pinch the fetlock to make him pick up his foot. If he does not lift it readily, very gently kick the hoof with the toe of your boot to make him do so. Hold the foot by the pastern slightly off the ground; run the point of the pick around the bottom of the foot where it meets the shoe and also around the *frog* (the triangular-shaped formation on the sole of the foot, which cushions the foot as it strikes the ground). Be sure not to poke the pick deeply into the sensitive cleft in the middle of the frog. Check the shoes for signs that new shoes are needed (see figure 60). Be sure there are no small stones lodged between the shoe and the foot, especially around or in the frog. Check the sole of the foot for signs of *thrush*. Extreme sponginess of the frog and a foul odor are the usual symptoms of thrush. If indicated, ask your blacksmith or vet to take a look.

Wipe out the dock area under the horse's tail with a sponge kept for that purpose alone.

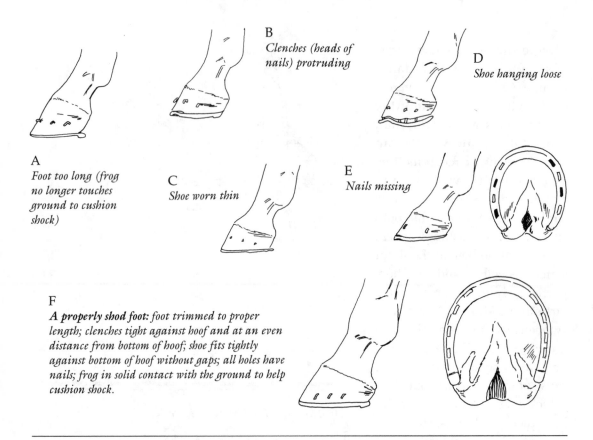

B
Clenches (heads of nails) protruding

D
Shoe hanging loose

A
Foot too long (frog no longer touches ground to cushion shock)

C
Shoe worn thin

E
Nails missing

F
A properly shod foot: *foot trimmed to proper length; clenches tight against hoof and at an even distance from bottom of hoof; shoe fits tightly against bottom of hoof without gaps; all holes have nails; frog in solid contact with the ground to help cushion shock.*

FIGURE 60:   *How to Tell if a Horse Needs Shoeing*

The horse's mane can be slicked down with a water brush. If it is thick and long, the mane can be pulled to a uniform length of four inches, which is customary for the hunter-type horses used for riding and jumping. Working from the underside of the mane—never the top—separate the hairs a few at a time and pull them sharply downward and out, using a metal mane comb in the other hand to assist the procedure.

The horse's tail can be left full, or its bottom can be *banged*—cut straight across. Be sure to cut the tail at least six inches or more *below* the hocks, never shorter. The horse will flatten his tail against his body when you cut it, but will carry it several inches higher when ridden. Consequently, a tail that looked a reasonable length when cut will suddenly rise to several inches above the hocks, instead of a few inches below. The horse also uses his tail to swat away flies; it is cruel to cut it too short for this purpose.

In England, the hairs on the horse's dock are frequently thinned by pulling; this practice is now becoming more popular in the United States, although most often the tail is left alone, or braided (plaited) for shows and sometimes for fox hunting (see figure 62, page 145).

In spring, when the horse sheds his winter coat, a *shedding blade* is useful. This is a strip of springy metal eighteen inches long with serrated teeth along one edge; it can be made into a loop by passing one end through a strap at the other. Use it gently all over the horse's body; do not use it on his head or his legs from the knees and hocks down.

In summer, a bath may be given to the horse after a ride. Use plain lukewarm water with no shampoo or soap, which dry the hair and skin. Usually two large buckets are needed to wash one horse, or you may use a hose instead. Rub the horse thoroughly with a large sponge and scrape off all excess water with a sweat scraper (either a straight aluminum one or the reverse side of the shedding blade). Walk the horse until he is dry. If there is any wind, cover him with a sheet or cooler. Never allow a wet horse to stand, as horses are vulnerable to colds and pneumonia.

The hooves can be painted with hoof dressing, available at tack shops; this moisturizes the sole and wall of the hoof. However, the dressing's attractive visual effect is short lived, as painted hooves pick up dirt and straw quickly.

In England, *wisping* is considered part of grooming: the horse's muscles are pounded rhythmically with a tightly woven, hand-sized pad of straw. This increases circulation and may improve muscle tone by causing the horse to flinch his muscles in anticipation of the next blow—a sort of involuntary isometric exercise for the horse. Those who practice wisping attribute to it improved muscle tone in the horse; others suggest that it may actually be of rather greater benefit to the muscles of the person wielding the wisp!

Clipping

A horse's winter coat is usually thick enough to keep him warm while he is standing still or slowly walking. If he is ridden with his thick coat, he becomes overheated and sweats. Wet hair is dangerous to a horse, especially in winter's sharp winds and cold temperatures, since horses are prone to pneumonia and respiratory ailments. So if you ride in winter, it is best to clip your horse and keep him blanketed.

Clipping upsets many horses and should be done by an expert. A *hunter clip*, leaving hair only on the legs and the saddle area, is the most usual clip in the United States. In England a *trace clip*, which removes hair from the underside of the neck and the sides and belly to the height of the traces of a carriage, is popular because the horse can be turned out and still be somewhat protected from the elements by the longer hair on his back and top side of his neck.

Clipped horses must be blanketed except when being ridden or turned out briefly to play. There is a special blanket called a *New Zealand rug* that is designed to be worn while the horse is in the pasture; a set of straps go around the horse's hind legs to hold it in place. For stable use, most people keep one blanket for night use—which soon becomes dirty on the outside from the stall's manure when the horse lies down to sleep—and another for day use.

Bandages

A word of caution about bandages: putting them on correctly is a practiced art, which you should learn from an expert, not a book. The consequences of applying bandages incorrectly are severe and may be irreparable.

There are two kinds: stretchy cotton *stockinette* bandages, about four inches wide, that tie with strings and usually come in bright colors; and *flannel* strips, six inches wide, usually gray or gray-blue, torn from a roll of material, and used over layers of white cotton. The latter are secured with special large safety pins, crossed in an X for added security, or with Velcro.

Correctly put on, both kinds are useful. Stockinette bandages used dry as work bandages while riding or *longeing* the horse can give support to the tendons; used wet they can soothe tired legs, hold a poultice in place, or smooth the hairs of the dock of the tail.

Flannel bandages are used during shipping to protect the horse's legs; they are also used in the stable to provide warmth and to support the tendons.

However, the danger in using any kind of bandage incorrectly should be noted. If work bandages come loose while riding, they can tangle around the horse's legs and cause him to fall. If they are too tight, the horse can *bow a tendon*—a condition of the tendon that runs along the back of the cannon bone when it "bows" out like the curve of a bow and arrow— causing irreversible damage and possibly permanent lameness. If they are tied incorrectly, they can cause painful contusions. If shipping bandages come loose while the horse is traveling, he may get tangled up in them and fall. An incorrectly attached safety pin can get lost in the stall and possibly be swallowed or cause a puncture wound. Learn from an expert, practice under guidance until you are sure of your ability to apply bandages correctly, and do not needlessly risk harming the horse.

Boots

I f your horse steps on the heels of his front feet with his hind feet, use *overreach boots*. If he cuts his feet or ankles by brushing his front or hind feet together as they pass, use *brushing boots*. Both are available at tack stores.

Braiding (Plaiting)

B raiding the mane and tail improves the appearance of the horse by making his neck look longer and finer and by showing off his hindquarters. Braiding for shows or hunting is best learned by observation and practice. The mane should be pulled to a length of

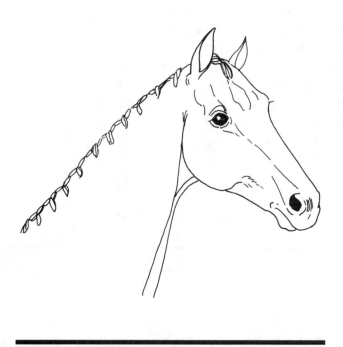

FIGURE 61: ***Braiding the Mane***

four inches before braiding (see the description in *Grooming*, page 137).

To braid the mane (see figure 61), first brush it with a wet water brush, then divide it with a mane comb into ten or twelve equal sections about one and one-half inches wide each. Divide each of these into three equal bunches. Try to make the braids lie as flat as possible. Braid each section so it is identical to the previous ones. That is, if you fold over the right-hand bunch first on one section, do so on each section. Roll or loop the braids under and sew them with heavy thread the same color as the mane. Rubber bands can also be used, but tend to look less neat than sewing. Colored yarn is sometimes used, but unless it is used expertly its color accentuates any unevenness. Braid and sew the forelock in the same way as the rest of the mane. When removing braids, cut the threads very carefully with small scissors, being sure not to cut the hair by mistake.

Braiding of the tail (which is braided only along the length of the dock) involves holding two sections of hair in each hand. The result should be a raised braid that runs the length of the dock.

Begin as high up as possible. Take a small bunch of hair from the right side, cross one from the left side just below it, and cross a third from the right side just below that (see figure 62). Bring the topmost bunch around and down to the middle of the cross formed by the other two, drawing in a few more hairs from the right side of the dock as you do so and merging them together with those already in your hand. Then take the next highest bunch, bring that down and around on the left side, adding to it a few hairs from the left side of the dock, and so on. When you reach the end of the dock, braid out the hairs to the end and curl them up to form a two-inch loop below the dock. Tuck the rest up inside the braided part of the dock and secure with a needle and thread.

Cleaning Tack

Tack should be cleaned daily to protect its leather and to prevent it from chafing the horse. Regular cleaning preserves good leather for a lifetime of use, and also gives you a chance to check for signs of wear. If any piece wears out, it could break while you are riding and cause an accident.

At the very minimum, the bit should be dunked in water as soon as it is removed from the horse's mouth, and the sweat washed from the parts of the saddle that touch the horse, including the girth. A saddle pad (numnah) should be allowed to dry, if damp, and brushed clean.

A thorough cleaning of tack is preferable. This is easier if you hang the bridle from a hook and place the saddle on a special sawhorse or saddle rack made for the purpose, which supports the saddle right side up, then reverses to hold it upside down for cleaning the bottom. Take apart the saddle and bridle. Wash each part separately with a large sponge and a pail of lukewarm water. Try not to soak the leather unduly, but be thorough enough to ensure that it is free of all sweat and caked dirt. If necessary, scrape it gently with a dull kitchen knife to remove built-up grime.

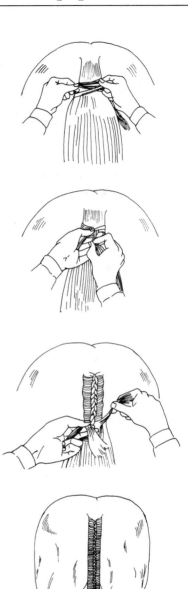

Hairs from bunch above are combined with new hairs.

FIGURE 62: *Braiding the Tail*

Dry the leather with a slightly dampened towel or chamois cloth. Rub in prepared saddle soap (the kind that comes in tin containers and resembles orange shoe polish), or Lexol or Neatsfoot Oil (liquid conditioners), or glycerin saddle soap (which comes in long bars), using a damp sponge. The leather should feel sticky when you finish; if the soap lathers as you rub it in, the sponge is too wet. Polish bits and stirrup irons with metal polish and rinse off the bit so the horse will not taste the polish. Reassemble the bridle and saddle.

Some new tack is pale tan in color and should not be used until it has been protected and darkened by frequent applications of Neatsfoot Oil or Neatsfoot Oil Compound. Small pieces, like parts of the bridle, may be submerged in Neatsfoot Oil and soaked for a couple of days; the saddle should be rubbed liberally with it for several days in a row, until it will not absorb any more. Wear old clothes when you ride for a while after breaking in new leather because Neatsfoot Oil can stain.

Store tack in a dry place away from direct heat. Moisture rots stitching and encourages mold to grow on leather; heat dries and cracks it. A properly ventilated tack room is the best storage place for tack not in use. Put a saddle rack at a convenient height on the wall, and hang the bridle nearby (some saddle racks have a hook for the bridle beneath). Keep a sturdy lock on the tack room door; unfortunately, there is a thriving black market in stolen tack.

QUIZ

1. Grooming is important for
   (A) stimulating circulation
   (B) improving appearance
   (C) checking for cuts or scrapes
   (D) all of the above

2. A thorough grooming should take place
   (A) before you tack up the horse
   (B) after you ride
   (C) both of the above

3. To pick up the horse's foot, stand facing
   (A) the horse
   (B) the same direction as the horse
   (C) the opposite direction as the horse

4. In the foot, sponginess of the frog and a foul odor are signs of
   (A) overwork
   (B) damp stable conditions
   (C) thrush

5. Signs that a horse needs to be reshod are
   (A) protruding clenches
   (B) shoes worn thin
   (C) a frog in solid contact with the ground

6. A banged tail should be cut
   (A) four inches above the hocks
   (B) six or more inches below the hocks
   (C) just below the dock

7. A horse may be given a bath
   (A) in summer after a ride
   (B) at any time of year
   (C) on windy days

8. Wisping means
   (A) stroking the horse gently with hand-fuls of straw
   (B) hitting the horse vigorously with a woven straw pad
   (C) tying up a hay bag at chest level

9. Clipping a horse in winter is necessary when
   (A) you plan to ride at more than a slow walk
   (B) you intend to go to horse shows
   (C) the horse is prone to girth galls

10. A New Zealand rug is a
    (A) kind of saddle pad
    (B) kind of blanket that can be used for turning out a horse
    (C) stable blanket

11. The main dangers in using leg bandages are that
    (A) they can slip down and tangle around the horse's legs
    (B) they can cause a bowed tendon if placed too tightly around the horse's legs
    (C) they cannot be used safely for shipping a horse in a trailer

12. When pulling a mane, you should pull the hairs from
    (A) the top of the mane so that only the under hairs are left
    (B) the underside of the mane
    (C) both of the above

13. Tack should be cleaned with
    (A) water as hot as you can stand it on your hand
    (B) lukewarm water
    (C) cold water

Answers: 1D, 2B, 3C, 4C, 5A,B, 6B, 7A, 8B, 9A, 10B, 11A,B, 12B, 13B.

12

Problems and Emergencies

Biting

Horses bite for a variety of reasons. A horse instinctively bites at those below him in the established pecking order. He may bite at and chew tack, clothing, or brushes because he's curious, or because he likes the taste or texture. If you approach a horse in the pasture, or while he is eating (especially grain), he may threaten to bite you knowing that your approach means the end of grazing and the beginning of work under the saddle. He may threaten to bite when his girth is being drawn up if he anticipates discomfort due to its being pulled up too sharply.

Biting at tack can best be prevented by simply keeping the tack out of the horse's reach.

Biting at people must not be tolerated whatever the reason. It is easy to cure if you make the correction so swift, forceful, and severe that the horse will not want to cross you a second time. At the first sign of bad temper, the horse should be punished; do not wait until he has actually taken a chunk out of you.

If a horse is a known biter keep a halter on him with a two-and-one-half-foot length of rope attached while he is in the stable and while he is turned out. At the first sign of an imminent bite—most horses flatten their ears back against their heads and look menacing—grab the rope, swat the horse hard with the flat of your hand just above the nostrils, on the side (where the skin is soft and there are no bones immediately beneath the surface), and holler loudly, "Hey, you!," or something else frightening. Then immediately *snatch* (jerk) down sharply on the rope two or three times, which will make the horse raise his head abruptly, and continue to holler at him. Make the whole experience short—five or six seconds at most—and traumatic. The horse will then bring his ears forward and assume a look of docility and concerned obedience, if not to say innocence. Keep an eye on him, however; most confirmed biters will wait until they think you have forgotten an incident and then try pinning their ears once again, just to see if they can get away with it. Repeat the cure—if anything, more severely than before. If the second correction is carried out sternly enough, a horse will usually amend his behavior thereafter for just a sharp "Hey!," at least from the person who corrected him. The process may have to be repeated by other people in order to make the horse mind his manners with everyone.

If the horse pins his ears while being ridden—past another horse, for instance—the correction is somewhat different. Give a sharp snatch on the reins and say "Hey!" to distract him from biting and make him pay attention. Snatching is most effective if you move your hands *forward* a split second before bringing them back, rather than trying to snatch from a position of light contact on the reins. Your hands must move not straight back, but rather on a diagonal line from the horse's mouth toward your chin. Do not spur or whip a biting horse when other horses are near; he will almost surely kick out if you do.

Kicking

In the stable or pasture, keep a halter and a short rope (two and one-half feet long) on a known kicker. If the horse shows any signs of anger (pinning of ears, lifting of one hind foot menacingly when you are leading, grooming, or handling him, snatch down sharply on the rope as described in *Biting*, above, and use a sharp word such as "Hey!" If a horse attempts to kick while being ridden, snatch the reins as you would for a horse who bites while being ridden.

Shying

If a horse becomes startled and *shies*, or jumps sideways, correct him with direct rein and the opposite leg. That is, if he shies away from something on his right, use right direct rein, moving your right hand to the right, and your left leg to push his body to the right. The left rein remains snugly against the horse's neck as a supporting rein.

Sometimes you can feel a horse begin to hesitate and tense his muscles in preparation for shying before he actually does so. If you feel this, urge him on before he has a chance to shy, using legs and, if necessary, whip. Maintain light contact with his mouth at all times if you suspect that he will shy.

If you suspect that a horse will shy away from a particular object, carry the whip in the opposite hand to encourage him to move away from the whip and toward the object that frightens him.

Bolting

If a horse "takes off" or *bolts* with you at the true flat-out gallop, he is in a state of panic and therefore thinking of nothing except running away from whatever frightens him. In this state his judgment is poor. You therefore need to take quick, decisive action.

First, try to steer him in the safest direction. Avoid traffic, sharp turns, ground with holes, and hard-surfaced roads. Head uphill, if possible, so as to

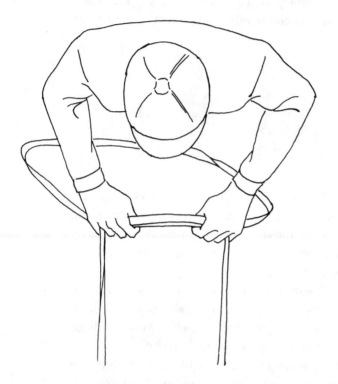

Holding reins in a full cross helps riders resist a horse who pulls.

FIGURE 63:   ***The Full Cross***

tire the horse out and slow him down. If the going is level and free of holes, and if there is ample space, you can then turn in a large circle, gradually making it smaller. But do not attempt this if the ground is slippery, likely to have holes, or if there is any possibility the horse may run into a fence, wall, or hedge, as a bolting horse may go through rather than over an obstacle.

The gallop of a bolting horse is, although rapid, actually very easy to sit to, being much more level than the canter. Most horses turn easily at the gallop if you use direct rein. Stay calm and gather your wits.

Be sure your feet are correctly placed in the stirrups and that there is no chance you will get hung up in them if you come off; have the stirrup on the ball or even the toe of your foot, but never pushed "home" (to the instep).

With your reins, form a bridge or *full cross* (see figure 63) by doubling the reins where they pass through your hands and holding the doubled part firmly with both fists. Shorten the reins so your hands are halfway up the crest of the horse's neck.

It is impossible to *outpull* a running horse. The usual aids for slowing from a canter will not work. You must, instead, *upset the rhythm* of the gallop so the horse cannot concentrate and cannot lower his head and neck as he would prefer. After his gallop stride is disrupted you can quickly slow him to the trot, and then to the walk, using the conventional aids.

To upset the bolting horse's rhythm, first move your hands *forward* to remove all pressure on the horse's mouth. Push your heels well down and three or four inches forward. Bracing against the stirrups, throw your shoulders and weight suddenly back. At the same time snatch (jerk) the reins as hard as you can, moving your hands slightly *upward* on a diagonal line from the horse's mouth to your chin, not straight back, and never downward. The horse needs to extend his head and neck down and forward to gallop strongly; by suddenly snatching the reins upward-and-backward, and shifting your own weight backward, you force him to move his front end up and his center of gravity back, and he cannot easily continue galloping. If necessary, repeat the snatch once or several times in rapid succession.

After you have stopped a bolting horse, if you have any doubts that you can control him, get off and lead him home. Any horse with a known tendency to bolt should be ridden with a standing martingale tightly adjusted and should not be ridden by a novice.

Balking

B*alking*, or refusing to go willingly forward, is a serious fault and if uncorrected may quickly lead to rearing. Correct a horse's slightest hesitation instantly, using leg or, if necessary, whip. Cease correction as soon as the horse moves forward. Sometimes riding just behind another horse can encourage a balky horse to follow. In severe cases, when the horse has learned that he can get away with balking, stronger correction is needed. In such cases, shorten the reins and hold them in one hand, hold the whip in a reversed position in your free hand, and give five or six sharp swats with the whip on each side, right behind your leg. If necessary, spurring on both sides may be added. Because stern correction may cause a balky horse to buck or attempt to rear, it should be undertaken only by an experienced rider.

Rearing

Rearing is a serious vice, as the horse may fall over backward with the rider under him.

The horse must be driven energetically forward at the first sign of rearing. Balking often precedes rearing, so proper correction of the former may prevent the horse from attempting to rear.

Once the horse is rearing, be sure *not* to put pressure on the reins, as he may react against it by rearing higher. Some people recommend pulling on one rein as soon as the horse's front feet return to the ground and forcing the horse to turn in a series of extremely small circles on the spot. Others recommend hitting the horse between the ears with a heavy object like a section of garden hose filled with sand. This may be effective in certain cases, but blows to the head are dangerous and may cause permanent damage. The best solution is prevention—never to allow a horse to become balky.

No novice should ride a horse that is known to rear. If you are not an experienced rider, get off at the first sign of rearing and walk the horse back to the barn. Let an expert correct rearing; the chances of getting hurt are too great for anyone but an experienced rider to attempt to cure it.

Ducking Out an Open Gate

If, while being ridden in a ring or arena, a horse tries to slip out an open gate as he passes it, carry the whip on the side nearest the gate and shorten the inside rein slightly. That is, if you are going counterclockwise, carry the whip in your right hand, and keep your left rein slightly shorter than your right. As he tries to slip out the gate to the right, tap his shoulder smartly and give a sharp dig with your heel on the side nearest the gate.

Always exit the ring by first *passing* the open gateway, then turning a loop to the inside of the ring to approach the gate head-on. If you invariably exit in this way, the horse will soon stop trying to duck out the gate as he passes it.

Stargazing

If a horse carries his head too high, he is said to be *above the bit*, or "stargazing." To bring the horse's head down, the rider must do two things. First, maintain forward movement. The horse must move willingly in front of your leg; if you find that squeezing with your calves does not produce an active response, use the whip just behind your leg hard enough so the horse will thereafter respond promptly to the light use of your legs alone.

Second, put light pressure on both reins equally, and gradually increase it until the horse seeks to do something to relieve the pressure on the bit. He will probably raise his head even higher. At this point, be very sure that he is moving actively forward, and then *raise your hands* until they are slightly higher than the horse's mouth. Instead of keeping a straight line from elbow to bit, bring your hands a couple of inches above this line (see figure 64). When the horse feels the upward pressure, he will try to avoid it by moving his head in the opposite direction. As soon as he makes any attempt to lower his head, even just a faint nod, soften the pressure on both reins immediately. If his head comes up again, repeat the process.

Incorrect: rider's hands too low. The more you pull down, the higher the horse will raise his head.

Correct: as the horse raises his head, rider raises hands slightly higher than horse's mouth, maintaining both active forward movement and pressure on the bit at the same time.

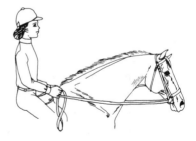

When the horse lowers his head, rider releases pressure on the reins.

FIGURE 64:   *Stargazing*

The key to this exercise is to maintain active forward impulsion. If this is lost, the horse may stop and possibly rear.

Pulling

Few things are less pleasant than a horse who habitually leans heavily on the bit, *pulling* against the reins. Some riders make the mistake of putting bits of greater and greater severity in the mouth of a puller, but the real solution to the problem is to ride a horse correctly, using a snaffle bit, and reschool him not to pull.

When a horse begins to lean on the bit and tries to increase his speed, put pressure on both reins equally, enough to be fairly unpleasant for the horse so that he will want to do something to make it go away. Do not jerk the reins, and do not arbitrarily increase and decrease the pressure. You may have to make the rein pressure quite hard at first, but do not ease up on it until the horse has slowed his pace. Then, and only then, soften the pressure on the horse's mouth by moving your hands forward momentarily or by opening your fingers briefly.

It is important to remember to *reward the horse as soon as he slows his pace, even though he may still be pulling against you,* as this tells him that he has done the right thing by slowing down. If you fail to reward him, he will soon realize that no matter what he does, the unpleasant rein pressure remains, and he will cease trying to relieve it.

As soon as you ease the pressure on the reins, a puller will usually speed right up again, and you must repeat the process, over and over until he finally realizes that you will always put a hard pressure on his mouth if he pulls and speeds up, but that he can remove this pressure by slowing down. As long as he remains in the slower speed, he finds that you put no pressure on his mouth (other than light contact with the bit). As soon as he picks up even a little speed and leans on the bit, however, he finds the pressure returns.

Most horses attempt to raise their heads when they encounter strong pressure on the bit. If this happens, raise your hands (see *Stargazing*, page 155) while you continue to maintain pressure on both reins. Be alert for the moment when the horse makes even a small attempt to lower his head—at first it may be an almost imperceptible "nod"—and reward his attempt; then immediately continue as before.

A good exercise to cure pulling is use of *transitions*, changes from one gait to another or to a halt, because this teaches a horse to slow down or halt properly on rein signal by using his hind legs. If a horse learns to halt on signal, he will not pull. Trot-to-halt transitions are especially good, because the trot is a two-beat gait and its speed and rhythm are easiest for the rider to judge. Moreover, few horses pull at the walk, while many pull too strongly at the canter to be easily corrected.

Most so-called "hard" mouths are really nothing more than the result of poor riding. A rider who pulls continually on the horse's mouth, even when he is going the proper speed, quickly teaches the horse that there is no escape from this punishment and no advantage in slowing down. In fact, the horse will try to go faster in an attempt to escape the pressure. A rider who pulls erratically against a pulling horse—by putting pressure on the reins, but then, because of either fatigue or ignorance, easing up on the reins while the horse is still going too fast—teaches the horse to pull by giving him confusing and arbitrary signals.

Taking the reins in a full cross (see figure 63, page 152) can help you resist a habitual puller better, as you can brace the crossed reins against the horse's neck and give some relief to your arms and shoulders without easing up on the reins.

Riding in Traffic

When you ride in a town or along a busy road, keep to the grass verge if there is one; otherwise, stay as close to the curb or the edge of the road as you can. Go in the same direction as traffic, and obey traffic signals as a car would. If your horse is frightened of noise, put his nose close to another horse's flank on the side away from traffic, being sure to choose a horse who is not inclined to kick. Thank drivers who slow down as they pass you with a friendly wave of your hand. Be alert for those who race by with horns blaring, however; maintain light contact with your horse's mouth, calming him with your voice. If you have any doubt of your ability to control your horse, ask an experienced rider to attach a lead to your horse's bit ring and lead him. Maintain light contact with your horse's mouth via the reins while the expert keeps your horse's head near his or her knee.

Do not trot or canter on hardtop roads, as they are both jolting and slippery, and can cause a broken leg if the horse slips and falls. Use hand signals to indicate your intentions to cars and to riders behind you. The left arm held straight out signals a left-hand turn; bent upward from the elbow, it signals a right-hand turn. A hand held up with the fingers apart signals a stop; call out "Hold hard!" just before you intend to stop, so riders behind you have a chance to stop also.

If you see a hole or broken glass, warn riders behind you by saying "'Ware hole!" or "'Ware glass!" (short for "beware") and pointing to the danger. Each rider in turn repeats the warning to the next rider.

You can sometimes check your position—see that your hands and legs are correctly positioned and that you are sitting up straight—by glancing at your reflection in the plate-glass windows of storefronts as you ride past, but be careful not to go too close to the buildings lest you annoy their owners.

Do not graze your horse beside busy roads, especially near railroad tracks. The grass along highways is filthy with car exhaust. Deadly herbicides have often been sprayed on it to keep down weeds, especially around railroad tracks.

Do not tie up your horse and leave him unattended; if he breaks loose near a road he could be hit by a car.

Use caution when strangers, especially children, ask to pat your horse. Even the best-mannered horse may accidentally nip if he thinks he is being offered something to eat. If you wish to let someone pat your horse, dismount and hold the horse so he does not step on the person, and show him or her how to pat the horse on the shoulder.

Do not ride after dark if you can possibly avoid it. If you must, wear a reflective vest or tie a large sash of reflective material over each shoulder and around your waist, and attach stirrup lights to your irons (these are available at tack shops).

Do not ride where you know you are not welcome: onto private property marked No Trespassing, across people's lawns, or near small children at play. Stay off streets where your horse's manure may cause concern, such as in certain residential areas. Be polite; you represent *all* riders to the general public. A courteous, friendly hello goes a long way toward building good will. Each year, with more and more shopping centers and superhighways and urban sprawl eating up the countryside, there are fewer places to ride. The willingness of the public to allow riders to use available land is directly influenced by their perception of riders. The person you speak to pleasantly may be the same one whose land you would like to ride across.

Riding Across Countryside

When you ride across country—over fields or through woods—remember that you are riding across someone else's property, and treat it with respect. Leave all gates exactly as they were when you came upon them; if they were shut, be sure they are securely fastened after you go through. If possible, all riders should wait while the last rider through closes the gate. If this is not practical then at least one person should wait with the last rider, to prevent his or her horse from panicking at being left behind.

If a dog chases your horse, a good tactic is to *call the dog to you* as you continue to ride, rather than trying to chase him away; the latter usually makes a dog more aggressive and persistent. Calling confuses and embarrasses him, and he will usually leave you alone thereafter. If your horse shows any sign of kicking out, snatch (jerk) the rein quickly, before he actually kicks, to remind him that it will not be tolerated.

If you pass through branches, hold them aside only long enough for you yourself to pass through. Do not try to hold them for the next rider; if you do, they will almost surely hit him or her squarely in the face.

Go around the edges of fields, not through them, as there is no surer way to guarantee that a farmer will forbid you access than punching tracks across his newly planted fields or frightening his livestock by riding among them. If you damage or hurt anything—a fence, an animal, or a field—tell the farmer at once and offer to pay for it. If a landowner tells you to leave, do not argue; offer your apologies politely, and depart.

If you are with a group, be sure that less experienced riders are not put in situations they are unable to handle. If one horse canters, usually the others will want to keep up with him. If someone in the group cannot canter confidently, he or she should first trot ahead with another rider, then let the rest of the group canter to catch up.

Do not gallop flat-out; the fastest you should go is a hand gallop, and that only if the ground is free of holes and the footing is good. If someone's horse bolts, do not gallop in pursuit; most horses will only run faster if pursued. Be sure that every rider knows how to stop a bolting horse, and that any rider who lacks the confidence or ability to ride alone is kept on a lead.

If you come to *panels* in a fence—lowered sections, solidly built, meant to be jumped, usually ten- or twenty-foot sections of a split-rail or other fence line— go over one rider at a time; those waiting their turn can circle at the walk or trot to keep their horses calm. If your horse refuses, punish immediately (see *Refusals*, page 134), but unless he then jumps at once, go to the end of the line and wait until the others have jumped before trying again. If your horse is not a confident jumper, follow another horse over, staying one or two horse's lengths behind. Do not go side-by-side with or half-a-length behind another horse, as the horse who is slightly behind will usually take off when the leading horse does and may have to make an enormous leap to clear the fence.

AT THE END OF THE RIDE

Walk the last half mile home, unless it is cold and raining or sleeting, in which case a slow jog-trot, just faster than a walk, is preferable. If the horse is the least bit overheated when you bring him to the stable, particularly in winter, loosen the saddle for a few minutes before removing it, then cover the horse with a sheet or cooler and walk him in hand until he is cool and dry. If the day is hot and he has sweated heavily, give him a couple of gulps of water at a time, walking him for one to two minutes between drinks, until he is "watered off" and doesn't want any more. Do not let a hot or thirsty horse drink a lot of water all at once after a ride.

Wait until he has had all the water he wants and is cool and calm before grooming (see Chapter 11) and feeding.

Accidents

By a very wide margin, most falls and horse-related mishaps result in nothing more than dented egos. But if there is an accident that seems serious to either horse or rider, emergency measures should be taken promptly.

If the rider has been knocked unconscious, been badly cut, or broken a bone, he or she should be kept quiet and warm with whatever clothing is at hand and, if possible, not left alone. Only leave an injured rider alone if it is otherwise impossible to get help. Do not leave the injured rider's horse alone or attempt to tie him up while you go to get help; if tied by the reins, he may break free. Instead, lead him with you.

After being knocked unconscious, a rider should not remount even if he or she claims to feel fine. The rider may have had a concussion, or he or she may faint once back in the saddle.

One person should go in search of a telephone. Call 911, tell the operator it is an emergency, and inform the hospital calmly and clearly of the location of the accident. Be sure to give the telephone number from which you are calling; let emergency personnel meet you there if you think that they will have trouble finding the scene of the accident unassisted.

If a horse has been knocked unconscious, call a veterinary clinic or hospital and follow their instructions exactly.

Lameness

There are many causes of lameness, involving in most cases strain, concussion of the foot on hard surfaces, poor shoeing, poor conformation, and, in some cases, too rich a diet. External factors such as mud, stones, or unclean stable conditions can also cause lameness.

It is important for every rider to recognize lameness and to know what to do about it. Unless the cause of lameness is known and a vet has advised exercise, the horse should not be ridden before the cause is found, treated, and eliminated.

Pain is always present in cases of lameness. Heat and swelling may or may not be evident. Most lameness occurs in the foot, because the weight of the horse's body is enormous in relation to the size of the hooves upon which this weight must be carried. Added to the burden of the horse's body weight is the stress caused by fast work at trot or canter, or by jumping on hard ground.

If, while riding, you suddenly notice unevenness in the horse's gait, especially at the trot (when unevenness is easiest to detect due to the even, two-beat nature of the trot), get off and inspect the sole of the horse's foot at once. If the onset of lameness was sudden, you may find that the problem is nothing more than a stone lodged in the angle created by the horseshoe and the sole of the foot, or in the *frog* (see figure 60, page 140). Use a sharp stick—or hoofpick, if you have one handy—to pry it out. Also check to see whether a shoe has pulled loose; if you can move the shoe at all with your hand, it is loose. Do not ride until a blacksmith resets the shoe.

If, however, the horse shows signs of lameness from the moment you begin to ride him (you will have picked out his feet before mounting, of course), then the problem is probably in the horse's leg or the foot itself. Lameness is most noticeable when the horse is first ridden, and will usually diminish or disappear altogether as he warms up. A veterinary examination will be needed to determine the cause.

Do not ride or jump a horse who is lame. To do so would be cruel, and could cause irreparable harm. Find out the cause and correct it without delay.

In some cases, corrective shoeing may be needed to compensate for irregularities in the horse's natural way of going; a horse whose conformation causes him to move incorrectly can become lame. A blacksmith can advise you about this.

HOW TO TELL IF THE HORSE IS LAME ON A FORELEG

Have someone trot the horse on a lead shank, leaving his head as free as possible, and move slowly downhill toward you. If the horse is sound, his head will not move up or down as he trots, but will remain perfectly still relative to his body. If he is lame, his head will appear to "nod" with each step. If lame on a forefoot, he will attempt to avoid putting weight on it by lifting his head up each time it touches the ground. For example, if he is lame on the left forefoot, he will raise his head as the left forefoot touches the ground and nod downward as the right (sound) forefoot touches the ground.

A second test is to have the person holding the horse turn him in tight circles first in one direction, then in the other. When the horse is forced to move in a circle one or two feet in diameter, lameness will be very apparent. That is, if the horse is lame on the left forefoot, he will step very uncomfortably when turned to the left, and will avoid keeping the left forefoot on the ground any longer than he has to.

HOW TO TELL IF THE HORSE IS LAME ON A HIND LEG

Have the horse trotted away from you, both uphill and downhill. Stand directly behind him and watch his croup. If he is lame on a hind leg, the croup will rise higher on the lame side than on the other side.

Then watch the horse as he is trotted past you in side view. Often the hind foot will step down less firmly than the sound foot.

WHO SHOULD DIAGNOSE THE CAUSE OF LAMENESS?

Good books on lameness do exist: *Veterinary Notes for Horse Owners*, by M. Horace Hayes, revised by J.F. Donald Tutt (New York: Arco, 1968), is among the best. But a beginner should not attempt to diagnose the cause of lameness unless that cause is readily apparent, such as a stone caught in the foot or a loose shoe would be. If a horse is lame, call the vet and get an expert opinion.

Ailments

A healthy horse looks bright and alert, eats well (with the exception of the habitually "picky" eater), and has no overt signs of illness. If a horse has a persistent cough, thinness, a dull "staring" coat, fever, or is unusually sluggish, seems uncomfortable and repeatedly gets up and lies down, has a runny discharge from nose or eyes, or seems weak or disoriented, call the vet and get an expert evaluation at once.

SIGNS THAT THE HORSE MAY BE AILING

Ask a vet to show you how to take a horse's temperature, and keep a thermometer on hand. A horse's normal temperature is 100.5 degrees Fahrenheit. One degree more is nothing to be concerned about and the temperature will usually soon return to normal. More than one degree above normal is cause for concern, and a veterinarian should check the horse. You should also call a vet if the horse appears dull, listless, and uninterested in food for more than a day; has a thick, yellowish nasal discharge; coughs persistently; has any abnormal swelling, particularly around the throat and beneath the jaw; stays thin and poor-looking despite eating well; or appears to be in obvious distress. The vet should also be called in the event of a cut, particularly a small and deep one such as a puncture wound, which can easily get infected if overlooked.

A horse who appears distressed, gets up and lies down repeatedly, and looks or nips at his flank, probably has *colic*. Colic is a general term for a number of stomach and intestinal disorders that are serious because horses lack the ability to regurgitate. The vet should be called immediately, as colic caused by a twisted intestine or impacting of grain can be fatal. The horse should be walked in hand until the vet arrives.

Every horseman and horsewoman learns over the years to recognize the symptoms of various ailments in horses. A novice should not attempt to diagnose or treat illness without direction from a veterinarian, but everyone should be alert for signs warning that a horse is ill, and should know when to call the vet. Get the names and telephone numbers of several veterinarians and keep them near a telephone for emergencies. The rule is: when in doubt, call the vet. It is better to err on the side of safety than to fail to get help and so lose a horse.

Fires

One rule must be observed without fail in all barns and stables: *No Smoking*. Never violate this rule, and do not hesitate to tell anyone foolish enough to smoke in a barn to stop immediately. As a further precaution against fires, electrical wiring must be checked periodically and all barns should be equipped with properly grounded lightning rods.

A horse's stall is his home. He associates it with food, peace and quiet, and comfort. In the event of a fire, with its smoke, shouting, and confusion, a frightened horse seeks shelter and naturally returns to his stall, even when the barn is aflame. Many horses die in fires each year, most often from smoke inhalation, to which they are acutely susceptible.

At the first sign of fire, if a telephone is nearby, call the fire department. Give the exact location and advise the best access to the barn for fire trucks. Then begin leading horses out of the barn with halters and lead shanks, starting with those in most imminent danger. If no telephone is close by, don't wait; begin to take the horses out at once. Seconds count. Tie a jacket or coat over each horse's eyes with the sleeve holes covering his ears because most horses, in their terror, refuse to leave the barn.

Talk calmly and confidently to reassure the horses. Be sure to lead them carefully so they do not bump into anything while blindfolded and become too frightened to move forward. If a horse balks, move him a step or two to the side, pushing against his shoulder to get him moving. If necessary, give a panicked horse a light kick in his ribs with one boot to get him moving again.

When a horse is well away from the fire, put him into a neighbor's barn, or a paddock or field where there is no chance he can break loose or jump out and return to the barn; you could also have another person hold him. If you must, tie him to a tree or fence; this should be a last resort, however, as a horse can usually break free when tied and is likely to try to do so.

When all horses are safe, call the vet to examine them for injury and smoke inhalation.

For an alphabetical listing of corrections to fifty problems that can occur while riding or handling horses, look at *Horse Sense: Cause and Correction of Horse and Rider Problems* by Kate Delano-Condax (Prentice-Hall/Simon & Schuster, 1990).

QUIZ

1. To correct a horse who bites, you should
   (A) use spurs
   (B) use a whip just behind your leg
   (C) smack the horse's nose with the flat of your hand

2. With a horse who bites, you should punish
   (A) after he actually bites
   (B) at the very moment he bites
   (C) at the first sign of bad temper

3. To correct a horse who bites while ridden,
   (A) snatch the reins
   (B) use a whip
   (C) use spurs

4. With a horse who shies, correct with
   (A) direct rein and opposite leg
   (B) direct rein and leg on the same side
   (C) indirect rein and opposite leg

5. If a horse bolts, the *first* thing to do is
   (A) steer toward a hedge or fence
   (B) try to turn in a large circle
   (C) steer the horse in a safe direction

6. To stop a bolting horse, you must
   (A) outpull him
   (B) tire him out
   (C) upset the rhythm of his gallop

7. Balking should be corrected by
   (A) turning in a small circle
   (B) reining back
   (C) driving forcefully forward

8. Rearing should be corrected by
   (A) anyone who is riding a horse who rears
   (B) an expert rider
   (C) a person on the ground

9. Kicking should be corrected by
   (A) spurs
   (B) a whip
   (C) a snatch on the reins

10. The correct way to exit from an open gate is
    (A) from an oblique angle as you pass it
    (B) a sharp outward turn as you pass it
    (C) turning to approach it head on after you have passed it

11. If a horse carries his head too high, correct it by
    (A) raising your hands and driving forward with your legs
    (B) lowering your hands and driving with your legs
    (C) using leg only, no rein, until he lowers his head

12. *True or false:* It is a good idea to let a horse have a few minutes' grazing along a road or railroad track occasionally to break up a long ride.

13. *True or false:* It is important *always* to be polite to the general public when you ride.

14. *True or false:* You should always ride the opposite direction from traffic; that is, facing it.

15. *True or false:* If a dog chases your horse, you are perfectly justified if your horse kicks at him.

16. *True or false:* As you ride through branches, it is best to hold them back for the next person.

17. *True or false:* If a rider is knocked unconscious, he should remount as soon as he feels all right.

18. *True or false:* At the end of the ride, you should always walk the last half mile home, regardless of the weather.

19. Most lameness occurs in the horse's
    (A) hind legs
    (B) forelegs
    (C) feet

(continued next page)

QUIZ

(continued)

20. If the horse suddenly goes lame while being ridden, suspect
    (A) tendon injury
    (B) a slipped stifle
    (C) a stone wedged in the frog or between frog and wall of the foot

21. To determine if a horse is lame on a foreleg, you should
    (A) canter him under saddle in small circles
    (B) trot him over small fences
    (C) have someone else trot the horse both toward and away from you

22. If a horse is lame on a forefoot, he will raise his head
    (A) as the lame foot touches the ground
    (B) as the sound foot touches the ground
    (C) neither of the above

23. If a horse is lame on a hind foot, you can determine which foot is affected
    (A) by watching the croup as the horse is trotted in hand away from you
    (B) by trotting the horse in small circles to left and right
    (C) by cantering up and down steep hills

24. A horse's normal temperature is
    (A) 98.6 degrees Fahrenheit
    (B) 100.5 degrees Fahrenheit
    (C) 100 degrees Celsius

25. If a horse gets up and down repeatedly, nips at his flank, appears distressed, and refuses to eat, suspect
    (A) worms
    (B) tetanus
    (C) colic

26. *True or false:* "When in doubt, call the vet" is the best policy.

27. When can you smoke in a barn or stable?
    (A) only when it has a cement floor
    (B) only if no combustible materials like hay or straw are nearby
    (C) never, under any circumstances

28. Before leading a horse from a burning barn, you should
    (A) call the fire department, no matter how far you must go to find a telephone
    (B) cover the horse's eyes with a jacket, placing his ears in the armholes
    (C) try to get help from anyone standing nearby

Answers: 1C, 2C, 3A, 4A, 5C, 6C, 7C, 8B, 9C, 10C, 11A, 12. false, 13. true, 14. false, 15. false, 16. false, 17. false, 18. false. 19C, 20C, 21C, 22A, 23A, 24B, 25C, 26. true, 27C, 28B.

Summary

HORSES ARE UNDENIABLY among the most beautiful animals in the world: generous, spirited, powerful, elegant in their movements, and sometimes even funny, with well-developed senses of humor.

Because horses are large animals, your experiences with them must be based on correct understanding of the right ways to handle, work with, and ride them. If you err in handling a parakeet, the consequences probably will not be of much significance. But with a horse weighing several hundred or a thousand pounds, the consequences of a serious error in judgment will be great. Therefore it is of more than passing importance that you learn correctly, right from the start.

What is "correct" is nothing more than what works best. Follow the instructions in this book carefully, and you will have a sound foundation for riding and handling horses safely and effectively.

This book is dedicated to Esther Wilson Perkins, my first riding teacher. Essie instilled in all of her students a sense of happiness, a sense of fair play, and a deep and abiding love of horses. Essie brought to riding an added dimension that is hard to define. It was a sense of being, for the moment, through the beauty and power of horses, closely connected to the universe. Horses can bring a special kind of joy to your life that is unequaled, to my mind, by anything else in the world.

Kate Delano-Condax Decker

1995

Index